AMMUNITION
FOR
PEACE-
MAKERS

AMMUNITION

FOR PEACE-MAKERS

Answers for Activists

Phillips P. Moulton

The Pilgrim Press
New York

The biblical quotations in this book are from the *Revised Standard Version of the Bible,* copyright 1946, 1952, and © 1971, 1973 by the Division of Christian Education, National Council of Churches, and are used by permission.

Library of Congress Cataloging-in-Publication Data

Moulton, Phillips P., 1909–
   Ammunition for peacemakers.

   Bibliography: p. 130.
   1. Peace—Religious aspects—Christianity.   2. War—
Religious aspects—Christianity.   3. United States—
Military policy.   I. Title.
BT736.4.M67   1986   261.8'73   86-91542
ISBN 0-8298-0732-2 (pbk.)

The Pilgrim Press, 132 West 31 Street, New York, NY 10001

To
Maurice McCrackin,
a true peacemaker

CONTENTS

ACKNOWLEDGMENTS

SPACE IS LACKING to acknowledge all of those who have read and criticized early versions of certain chapters or who have provided me with information and encouragement. Special mention, however, is due to my wife Mary; my son and daughter, Larry and Kathy; and the following: Melvin Beckman, Richard Birdsall, Kenneth Boulding, Mary Carry, Larry Erickson, Carol and W.H. Ferry, Abraham and Ida Kaufman, Doug and Pat Lent, Brad Lyttle, Robert Rumsey, Robert Simpson, John K. Stoner, Joe Volk, and Carlton Wells.

A preliminary version of the first chapter was delivered as the presidential address to the American Academy of Religion, Midwest Section, and at an annual gathering of Friends General Conference. Portions were presented also to the Peace and Justice Colloquium of the Earlham School of Religion, the Military Study Group at the University of Michigan, the Lansing Chapter of the Womens International League for Peace and Freedom, and a symposium of the Middle Atlantic Region of the American Friends Service Committee. The book has profited from the critical comments of participants on those occasions, not all of whom, to be sure, share my own views.

Thanks are due to James Shackelford, Dorothy Foster, and Janet Rose for efficient research and expert typing. Acknowledgment is also extended to Pendle Hill Publications for permission to include the substance of some paragraphs from one of my Pendle Hill Pamphlets. I am especially grateful for the friendly and efficient assistance of staff members of the United Church Board for Homeland Ministries, notably Marion M. Meyer, senior editor, who spent many hours making the manuscript more incisive and readable.

INTRODUCTION

NEARLY ALL AMERICANS share the same yearning—for lasting peace. Yet we differ on how to achieve that elusive goal. A major point of difference concerns the size and role of the military establishment considered necessary for national security.

We may distinguish two broad approaches to this issue. One is typified by the administration of President Reagan and the Committee on the Present Danger—advocates of a huge military buildup. The phrase "peace through strength" generally refers to a high degree of military readiness characteristic of this first approach, and is so used in the chapters that follow. Yet those who advocate the second approach consider their active pursuit of peace and proposals for defense as also exhibiting strength, although of a different sort.

The second approach is taken by those who favor deep reductions in our military program, coupled with a range of initiatives and agreements aimed at alleviating tension with the Soviet Union. Most of these would support what they term "an adequate military defense," but at a level so much lower than the first group as to constitute an alternative policy. The Center for Defense Information and many liberal Democrats belong in this category. Sharing this approach for the immediate future and advocating the same alternatives to the first approach are those, small in number, who favor eventually going further. They would replace the whole military system with nonviolent, civilian-based defense, using the sort of tactics employed by Mahatma Gandhi and the Polish Solidarity movement.

It is unfortunate that those on both sides of this issue talk past each other. Each side fails to deal directly with the views of those in the other camp. Since I belong in the second group, favoring a greatly reduced emphasis on the military, this book is not an impartial presentation of both sides. Yet I try to state the opposite position clearly and fairly while indicating its inadequacy. Although I hope some of the first group will be venturesome and open-minded enough to read this book, my primary aim is to provide the second group with the "ammunition" needed to address the main issues.

As the Table of Contents indicates, I focus on the major points where the two sides differ. I believe no other book provides the general reader with comprehensive answers to these same questions. Keenly aware of the many contemporary books on war and peace, I have discussed only briefly, or not at all, the facts and ideas that have become widely known. For example, no elaboration is needed on the devastating effects of nuclear war or the desirability of peace. I have tried to bring to a focus the ideas dealt with in fragmentary fashion by others and to concentrate on areas that others tend to ignore. Because the book is not intended primarily for specialists, I have kept technical details to a minimum. The works in the bibliography were chosen according to essentially the same criteria.

The European and American peace movements have achieved a real breakthrough in raising public awareness of our increasing peril. They have had some effect on the policymakers of Western Europe and the United States. Yet a disturbingly large number of people still support the arms buildup. As long as they believe that the Soviet Union is intent on attacking the United States or Western Europe, to be deterred only by massive arsenals, they will not be likely to hear what the rest of us have to say. As one observer writes of the Pentagon officials, "The demonstrations of mass feeling have been brushed off like some annoying insect." Lest our efforts and proposals seem irrelevant to those in the first camp, we need to deal thoroughly with what they consider the main issues.

A well-informed scientist recently made a vivid presentation to a group of business men and women on the consequences of nuclear war. Because the effects would be so disastrous, he insisted that the United States should stop adding to its nuclear arsenal. His listeners appreciated the presentation and did not challenge its accuracy. But during the question period, it was apparent that they were not persuaded that the nation should drop out of the arms race. They kept asking about the Russians: Could the speaker give a talk like that in Moscow? What about our freedoms? What about the USSR arms escalation? Weren't the Russians hell-bent for world domination? When his answers failed to satisfy them, he became frustrated. Here he was, telling them how catastrophic nuclear war would be, and instead of jumping on the bandwagon for peace, they were asking about the Russians!

On another occasion, a prominent religious leader lectured to a university audience on the need to oppose certain weapons systems. Then someone asked him about deterrence. He brushed it off with the remark that it was a dead issue, not to be taken seriously. Yet practically every rationale for U.S. foreign policy stresses deterrence—the concept that military might is needed to deter a potential aggressor from launching an attack. The speaker failed to meet the questioner where the questioner was.

The assumptions of those who advocate "peace through strength" may seem plausible until they are examined closely. For example, some time ago a group of children was taken to the White House to express their fears and concerns for the future. To their simple, eloquent plea for peace—for a chance to grow up in a warless world—the President had a ready response. He sympathized with them and promised to do everything possible to increase our military strength. This, he assured them, would protect us from the Soviet threat.

A few weeks later, a delegation of physicians warned the President of the impossibility of providing adequate medical treatment to nuclear war survivors. He replied in similar fashion: we will keep the peace by enlarging our nuclear stockpiles. He added that we need not worry; our policy of deterrence has prevented war for four decades.

When Americans in nationwide referendums endorsed a weapons freeze and arms reduction, the President announced that he favored even more drastic reduction. To accomplish this, he declared, we must bargain from strength. Therefore, we will deploy MX, Pershing II, and cruise missiles, build more nuclear-armed submarines, and militarize outer space!

Concerned economists criticize the massive U.S. military budget; they point out that it increases inflation and unemployment and causes hardship for the poor and elderly by diverting funds from social welfare programs. All very true. But if policymakers are convinced that nuclear war or a fearsome Soviet takeover can be prevented only by increasing our military might, they reason logically that we have no choice— we must endure whatever sacrifices are necessary to avoid such disasters.

Those of us who propose genuine, deep arms reduction can support our position with facts, logic, and common sense; but we must deal directly with the assumptions behind the replies given to the children, the physicians, the voters, and the economists. We need to grant whatever validity these replies have and then show that nuclear weapons are more provocative than deterrent, that the Soviet threat can be cut down to size, that genuine arms reduction becomes *less* likely as we enlarge our arsenals, and that, lucky as we have been for forty years, we cannot expect to live much longer if we continue our present course.

We need also to challenge the morality of preparing to slaughter millions of our fellow human beings. Finally, we need to show that with a different attitude, we can take immediate steps to reduce the threat of nuclear war and develop an alternate method of defense for the future that will eliminate the threat. This book aims to meet these needs—to provide new ammunition for the struggle to achieve a sound alternative to the policy mistakenly labeled "peace through strength."

Chapter I.

DETERRENCE DOES NOT WORK— STRENGTH BRINGS WAR

EVERYONE WANTS PEACE. Yet we multiply nuclear weapons. Why? The chief reason given for building and maintaining military might is that it provides national security. By threatening retaliation, its alleged purpose is to deter potential enemies from attacking us. This is the policy of deterrence, or "peace through strength." "To deter successfully," writes Secretary of Defense Caspar Weinberger, "we must be able—and must be seen to be able—to respond to any potential aggression in such a manner that the costs we will exact will substantially exceed any gains the aggressor might hope to achieve."[1] Since World War II, states Weinberger, this has been the "cornerstone of our strategic nuclear policy." It is repeatedly referred to as such in official Department of Defense reports.[2]

This chapter refutes the doctrine of deterrence and shows that escalating our military power does not increase our security and, to a large extent, is done for other reasons. Although I shall focus on nuclear deterrence, much that follows applies also to deterrence with conventional weapons.

Advocates of deterrence are not warmongers. They may oppose the development of first-strike weapons and plans to fight and "win" a protracted nuclear war. Many of them favor a bilateral nuclear freeze, followed by genuine arms reduction and the eventual elimination of nuclear weapons. But they believe that until that occurs, maintaining the ability to retaliate with nuclear weapons is the best way to prevent war.

As we examine the pros and cons of nuclear deterrence policy, we should note this anomaly: It depends on threatening an act that would annihilate us if we did it. We seek to avoid using nuclear weapons by resolving to use them under certain conditions. If deterrence fails and we are attacked, to escalate the madness by retaliating would ensure our own destruction. Yet decision-makers and military personnel are programmed to do just that. This basic contradiction should be enough to condemn the policy. Yet it seems not to have destroyed its credibility. After all, military history is replete with irrational and suicidal acts. If deterrence works and the weapons are never used, the problem vanishes. If deterrence fails, we are doomed. Hence the question before us is whether, and to what extent, it does work.

CONDITIONS FAVORABLE
TO DETERRENCE

There is some truth in the concept of deterrence. If nation A is heavily armed, a potential attacker, B, will doubtless take this into account. Other effects of A's military machine must be considered, however. Very likely it provoked B to create the arms buildup that now constitutes a threat. In that case, the arsenal of A merely deters, to a limited degree, the very danger it created.

Only under certain conditions is military strength more deterrent than provocative. One such situation may exist, temporarily, when a nation or alliance has such overwhelming military dominance that none can rival it. A different type of deterrence prevails when a nation poses no threat to others— when its military strength is solely defensive—so that other nations feel no need to attack it for the sake of their own security. Present-day Switzerland is an example. In such a

2

case, the potential aggressor is deterred not by the threat of retaliation, but by the prospect of being thwarted by the defense. Whether it is retaliatory or defensive, a third requirement of deterrence is that no arms race be in process or in prospect. The existence of an arms race shows that neither side has been deterred.

As we reflect on these conditions, we recognize, first, that no nation or alliance now has a clear preponderance of strength. Henry Kissinger has rightly pointed out that deterrence for the United States was seriously eroded when we lost our atomic monopoly.[3] Furthermore, nuclear weapons are not solely defensive; they are more suited for offense than defense. As a consequence, rival nations have ample reason to fear one another and so to contemplate a preemptive strike. And the arms race speeds along. Thus it seems evident that the conditions generally favorable to deterrence no longer exist among major powers.

Yet nuclear weapons would function as a deterrent in one type of situation. Let us assume that the policymakers in the United States or the Soviet Union were deliberating in the absence of a crisis or confrontation, and that they were completely rational and had ample time for reflection. Assume also that, believing peaceful coexistence over the long term to be extremely unlikely, they were considering a first strike. At the same time, they knew that however massive their attack, the opponent would still have enough nuclear capability to obliterate their entire nation.

In such circumstances, the nuclear weapons of the opponent would have a deterrent effect. The decision-makers would think twice before launching an attack. This is the element of truth in the doctrine of deterrence. It is the one scenario that appears to justify the motto of the Strategic Air Command: "Peace Is Our Profession." A more realistic analysis, however, reveals that, everything considered, military escalation increases, rather than decreases, the likelihood of war.

LIMITATIONS AND DEFECTS
OF DETERRENCE STRATEGY

In every field of endeavor, we tend to think in habitual patterns that have been tolerably satisfactory in the past. When a radically new situation arises, it is not easy to make the adjustments needed to deal with it effectively. It is not surprising, then, that many arms analysts and policymakers retain a mind-set that is too narrow for the age of thermonuclear weapons. Adhering to traditional patterns of thought and action, they repeat slogans based on assumptions that will not always stand the test of careful examination. Concentrating on the deterrent effect of nuclear weapons in the one type of situation just described, these analysts ignore more significant, dangerous effects.

This has been noted by at least one member of the defense bureaucracy, Fred Iklé, undersecretary of defense for policy: "Those calculated decisions which our deterrent seeks to prevent are not the sole processes that could lead to nuclear war. . . . The approach now prevailing puts almost all effort into preventing the 'rational' decision."[4] The crucial question is not whether military might has *any* deterrent effect, but rather, What are its *total* effects? To get a comprehensive picture, the positive needs to be balanced against the negative. When this is done, it becomes evident that in today's world, military might is more provocative than deterrent.

1. Survival not always considered the highest value. A basic weakness in the deterrence theory is its lack of realism in assuming that the rival nation will place survival above all other values—that the fear of destruction will prevent it from attacking. Other motives or considerations may outweigh survival. For example, a jingoistic sense of national honor or a false concept of patriotism could easily take precedence. So could a deep sense of injustice or religious fanaticism.

Attempting to justify the deployment of additional nuclear weapons in West Germany, Alexander Haig referred to

4

values that he ranked above survival. He told a Berlin audience: "Democracy and the rule of law . . . are things worth fighting for."[5] To do so with nuclear weapons, however, would destroy not only West Germany, but probably also the United States and perhaps all humankind.

A nation may launch an attack and accept the risk of destruction out of sheer desperation if it thinks that its situation is intolerable or deteriorating seriously. It is then ranking higher than survival the values it is lacking or thinks it is losing. Among these may be its economic well-being or its status among nations. Japan attacked Pearl Harbor when it felt encircled and economically constrained by the West and feared that the Western powers would cut off its access to vital raw materials. It was willing to risk defeat on the chance that it could preserve or gain certain values. It was not deterred by the superior industrial and potential military strength of the United States.[6]

The deterrence doctrine rests on the assumption that the fear of destruction will prevent a leader from launching an attack. But any one of several motivating factors could outweigh that fear. Arms strategists provide us with no answer to this criticism.

2. Decision-makers not always thoroughly rational. A second weakness in the deterrence theory is its assumption that the decision-makers of *all* nuclear powers will *always* be thoroughly rational. This is wishful thinking. It fails to recognize how irrational people are much of the time. Those who have probed deeply into human nature, like Sigmund Freud and Reinhold Niebuhr, confirm abundant human experience in this regard. Within a few years, additional nations will be able to produce the bomb. Can it be assumed that all their leaders will invariably be guided by reflective and thoroughly realistic judgments?

The macho reaction would be a probable cause of war. Decision-makers may be driven by the desire to appear tough, to avoid being labeled appeasers, by unwillingness to

5

back down when faced with an ultimatum. This powerful human tendency could cause a leader to risk catastrophe rather than lose face in the eyes of peers and constituents. During the Cuban missile crisis, this was apparently a factor in the refusal of President Kennedy's advisers to consider seriously Adlai Stevenson's proposal for a compromise solution.[7]

When Admiral Hyman Rickover commissioned the first Trident submarine, with its 192 nuclear warheads and total explosive power of 2.4 million tons of TNT, he exulted that it would strike "fear and terror in the hearts of the enemy."[8] Common sense tells us that terror and anxiety are not conducive to rational thought and action. This is confirmed by the studies of psychologists and sociologists.[9] The more we threaten the Soviet leaders, the less secure they become; in response, they threaten us more, making us less secure. In today's world, the only true security is shared security.

Note this contradiction: Deterrence is based on the assumption that a potential opponent will be thoroughly rational; yet the military threat that is supposed to be the deterrent creates insecurity that breeds irrationality. Our policymakers have not dealt adequately with this contradiction.

Such factors as emotional strain, fatigue, drug usage, or mental instability could also distort rational judgment enough to set missiles flying. In *Thirteen Days*, his memoir of the Cuban missile crisis, Robert F. Kennedy writes:

> *The strain and hours without sleep were beginning to take their toll. . . . Each one of us was being asked to make a recommendation which would affect the future of all mankind. . . . That kind of pressure does strange things to a human being, even to . . . mature, experienced men. . . . The pressure is too overwhelming. . . . Some . . . even appeared to lose their judgment and stability.*[10]

3. Human error or miscalculation could trigger war. In addition to the irrational decisions and errors that could result

6

from the factors just mentioned are the miscalculations that people make even under the best conditions.

In the name of deterrence, we pile up more nuclear weapons, disperse them more widely, and deploy them in more threatening situations. "Peace through strength" we proclaim. But this method of keeping the peace depends on no one making a crucial error in judgment or communication—or miscalculating the motives or reactions of potential enemies. Yet a common thread running through studies of wars and international crises is that miscalculations are often involved in their origins and escalation. Hugh Henning, director of the British Atlantic Committee, has rightly pointed out the miscalculation by the aggressor at the start of both world wars.[11] The aggressors thought they could get away with actions that rivals were determined not to allow.

Richard N. Lebow, professor of government at Cornell University, has made a thorough study of thirteen occasions when policymakers engaged in brinkmanship—actions that entailed the risk of war. These included, for example, the Russian challenge of Japan in 1903–4 and the Cuban missile crisis in 1962. In eight of these cases, available evidence showed the odds to be against success. Noting that the judgment of the decision-makers was "more often than not erroneous," Lebow concluded, "Our empirical findings raise serious questions about the utility of deterrence."[12]

4. Technical malfunction could precipitate war. A fourth unrealistic aspect of the deterrence doctrine is its fantastic optimism in assuming that no technical or mechanical failure will trigger a holocaust. Innumerable false alarms have occurred over the past twenty years. In response, U.S. bombers have warmed up, tactical fighter aircraft have been launched, intercontinental ballistic missile units have gone on alert, and, in at least one instance, a command and control plane took off to direct operations.[13] In each case, it took from three to six minutes of frenzied checking to determine that no Soviet

7

missiles were en route. (Reliable information is lacking regarding the nature and frequency of similar occurrences on the Soviet side.)

5. *A combination of factors could touch off a war.* One might well ask why miscalculations or errors have not yet produced a nuclear war. One reason is that our officials have done a good job of creating redundant safety devices and measures that reduce the risk. On this basis, government spokespersons keep assuring us that unintended war is unlikely. They fail to note that war could erupt from a combination of factors during a military confrontation between the United States and the Soviet Union. If a series of false alarms had occurred during a major crisis, we would probably not be here today.

Reports published in October 1984 by experts in relevant fields who make up the Working Group on Unintentional Nuclear War of the International Physicians for the Prevention of Nuclear War (IPPNW) summarize the danger: "We live with the unacceptable high risk of inadvertent nuclear war, and . . . this risk is increasing." After listing several reasons for this, such as the lack of effective U.S.-USSR communications and crisis management programs, they emphasize the impossibility of preventing every type of malfunction. They note that precautions and safety devices that are apparently adequate for every conceivable situation may not be adequate for a series of inconceivable coincidences.

They cite the power blackout in the northeastern United States and Ontario in 1965 and the accident at the Three Mile Island nuclear power plant in 1979. In each case, many precautions had been taken in the system design. After the power blackout, it was claimed that modifications made it impossible for such an accident to occur again. But in July 1977, a succession of lightning strikes that "just never happen" (to quote the president of Consolidated Edison Company) knocked out the New York part of the system. The IPPNW Working Party concludes: "The most significant risk . . .

8

seems to come from the possibility of a combination of an international crisis, mutually-reinforcing alerts, and possible computer failure and human error."[14]

It should be emphasized that the arms buildup largely responsible for the danger of unintended war is invariably rationalized by reference to the doctrine of deterrence. For example, many of the U.S. nuclear weapons are designed at the Lawrence Livermore National Laboratory in California. The former public affairs director of the laboratory states that the scientists are "sharp people . . . very competitive with the laboratory at Los Alamos." It is in their interest "to be very creative about the kinds of weapons they come up with so that they get more contracts." They prefer not to be pictured as being in the weapons business, but when asked about it, they give the standard reply: "We're involved in deterrence. . . . The only way to achieve peace is . . . from a position of strength." (When the public affairs director came to realize that he and his colleagues were deceiving themselves, he resigned.)[15]

Although a few defense policymakers have given lip service recognition to the increasing dangers attendant on our deterrence strategy, they have not halted the escalation of nuclear weapons, nor have they offered any effective solution to this problem.

6. *Military power more provocative than deterrent.* We have noted that the dominant U.S. policymakers and defense analysts think within a narrow range of traditional assumptions that do not take adequate account of the radically different situation that nuclear weapons have thrust upon us. This is especially evident when one considers the whole range of effects of the arms buildup. On the surface, it seems obvious that increasing U.S. military strength would deter potential aggressors. In a limited sense, perhaps it does. But it also has a provocative effect, which our leaders ignore. The primary question, then, is whether the provocation outweighs the deterrence.

9

Surprisingly, the advocates of military escalation as a deterrent scarcely consider how the Soviet Union will react. Piling up additional nuclear weapons does not increase U.S. security, for we are not alone in doing so. Our action provokes the Soviets to match or surpass us. It accelerates a dangerous arms race. Far from constituting a deterrent, the result is that each side is less secure than it was before.

In October 1981, President Reagan outlined a massive military expansion program. One of our most perceptive and loyal public servants, Paul C. Warnke, former director of the Arms Control and Disarmament Agency, testified before the Senate Foreign Relations Committee concerning that program. He made this astute observation:

> *In deciding on a new weapons system, we ought always to ask ourselves how we'll feel when the other side does the same, as they are sure to do. In deploying multiple independently targeted reentry vehicles in 1969, we exploited a temporary technological edge. But if MIRVed missiles had never been deployed, we would not today have any concerns about possible ICBM vulnerability. Before going ahead with sea-launched cruise missiles, we ought to consider a future time when we might have to regard every Soviet trawler or fishing boat as a strategic nuclear delivery vehicle. And I doubt that we could ever know, or devise a verification formula to count, the numbers of Soviet warheads on a sea-launched cruise missile force.[16]*

A proposal to ban MIRVs (Multiple Independently Targeted Reentry Vehicles) and cruise missiles instead of developing them would almost certainly have been accepted by the Soviets: their technology was behind ours; their overburdened economy needed relief; they have a realistic fear of the holocaust such weapons bring closer.

U.S. deployment of ever more speedy and accurate nuclear weapons incites the Soviets to threaten us in like fashion. As the readiness to strike intensifies on both sides and a crisis develops, suppose the strategists of one side conclude that war is imminent. They then face two alternatives: if they hesitate, they will risk the unimpaired might of the enemy. If they strike first, they will greatly reduce the opponent's destructive power. They will have a tremendous incentive to launch a preemptive attack. "Use them or lose them" will be the cry. The other side will react in similar fashion, producing the scenario posed by Thomas C. Schelling, professor at the Kennedy School of Government, Harvard University: "He, thinking I was about to kill him in self-defense, was about to kill me in self-defense, so I had to kill him in self-defense."[17]

Defense analysts stress our "resolve" to use nuclear weapons. The emphasis is unnecessary. The Soviets know only too well that we used them on defenseless civilians merely to hasten the victory that was already within our grasp.[18] They have every reason to fear that no moral scruples would prevent us from using them again. We have repeatedly threatened to do so.[19] Because our newer weapons are especially suited for a first strike, it would scarcely be surprising if they seek to beat us to the punch.

George Kennan, former ambassador to the Soviet Union, has pointed out that the only real *incentive* for the Soviets to bomb the United States would be the weapons deployment with which we threaten them.[20] Yet we claim that this enormous striking power is meant to deter such an attack! The *ability* of the Soviets to attack is provided by what they insist is only a deterrent—their nuclear arsenal. The paradox is that the more we build up our so-called deterrent, the more provocative it becomes. Recognizing this, Kennan has expressed the thought of many perceptive students of U.S. foreign policy: "If we Americans had no nuclear weapons whatever on our soil instead of tens of thousands . . . now . . . deployed, I would feel the future of my children and grandchildren to be far safer than I do at this moment."[21]

This is relevant also to the deployment of intermediate-range nuclear missiles in Western Europe. Christopher Paine, arms control staff member of the Federation of American Scientists, warns: "The very act of dispersal could prompt the attack these weapons are supposedly designed to deter."[22]

11

Hence comes the resounding "No!" that is heard from the common people of Europe.

Several scientists and other scholars who constitute the Boston Study Group have made a thorough study of U.S. defense needs and expenditures. They published their findings in 1982 in a carefully researched volume, *Winding Down: The Price of Defense*. Although not advocating the total abolition of U.S. nuclear weapons, they contend that "a strong case can be made that keeping nuclear weapons invites attack more than it inhibits one. . . . War today is in fact itself risked by the very preparations which we are told are made in the interest of defense."[23]

7. Vertical proliferation stimulates horizontal proliferation. In still another way, seeking deterrence by enlarging our nuclear stockpiles increases the danger of war more than it prevents it. It encourages additional nations to get nuclear weapons. The reasons for this are evident.

After all, if nuclear weapons allegedly provide peace through strength for the United States, why should this not be true for others? President Saddam Hussein of Iraq has openly declared that the Arabs need the bomb for this very purpose.[24] And just as the United States is now accumulating nuclear weapons not only to deter, but also to initiate or fight a war, if deterrence fails, Third World nations naturally conclude that such weapons would also be useful in actual combat.

Moreover, the very possession of nuclear arms by the major powers gives the weapons a prestige value in the eyes of smaller nations. The first nuclear explosion by France was welcomed by Charles de Gaulle with the boast that France became "stronger and prouder" that day.[25] As Bernard Goldschmidt, who publicized the technology of reprocessing plutonium, declared, "If you wanted to be somebody in this world, you had to have a bomb."[26]

It is ironic that trying to prevent war by supposedly improving our nuclear deterrent actually has the opposite effect. In respect to proliferation, the technology that brings smaller, cheaper weapons makes it easier for other nations to manufacture them. Our development of cruise missiles, for example, provides the know-how for nations that could not afford the larger, more expensive rockets.

At the high-level Stanley Foundation Conference on Non-Proliferation in 1980, twenty-four statesmen and scholars from sixteen nations explored the reasons for the spread of nuclear weapons (horizontal proliferation) and possible methods of arresting that spread. They traced the major reason to vertical proliferation (the expansion of nuclear arsenals by the superpowers).

In the Non-Proliferation Treaty of 1970, the major powers agreed to reduce, and eventually eliminate, their nuclear arsenals, while the nonnuclear states ageed not to develop them.[27] The failure of the superpowers to fulfill their pledge gives the smaller nations a compelling excuse for pursuing dreams of nuclear glory. This became evident at the second Non-Proliferation Treaty Review Conference in late 1980. As former President Carter has declared: "We have little right to ask others to deny themselves such weapons . . . unless we demonstrate meaningful progress toward the goal of control, then reduction, and ultimately, elimination of nuclear arsenals."[28]

The continuation of the arms race, especially by the United States and the Soviet Union, is done ostensibly for deterrence. Whatever deterrent effect it has, however, is more than offset by the increasing likelihood of nuclear war brought on by proliferation. As more nations get the bomb, the world becomes more explosive. "Peace through strength" is a high-sounding slogan, but creating that strength—because of its effects on other nations—brings us closer to war.

8. Summary of limitations. The preceding discussion reveals the irony of the concept of deterrence, on which U.S. foreign policy is allegedly based. It is probably true that the massive stockpiling of nuclear weapons tends to deter a rational ruler from starting a war when there is ample time for reflection and no crisis exists. But that is the least likely way a

13

nuclear war might start. Strengthening nuclear capabilities to guard against that one unlikely scenario greatly increases the probability of war starting in other ways.

Despite allegedly deterrent arsenals, national leaders may start a war because of one (or a combination) of these factors:

- They believe that values more important than survival are at stake—national honor, patriotism, freedom, justice, or religion.
- They do not always act rationally. Their decisions may be affected by macho reactions, fear, anxiety, and other emotional factors.
- Human errors and miscalculations become more likely as nuclear weapons become more numerous and complex.
- Technical or mechanical failures could produce misleading signals, or a computer error in a launch-on-warning system could set missiles flying.
- The buildup on one side provokes similar action by the adversary, increasing the likelihood of a dangerous confrontation.
- The proliferation of nuclear weapons gives to additional nations the means to wage a disastrous war, which could involve the superpowers.

What defense strategists overlook is that the possible deterrent effect of nuclear striking power is far outweighed by the increasing peril it creates. If we removed the deterrent, the Soviets would almost certainly remove theirs (see chapter III). Our world would then be much safer.

FUNCTIONS OF MILITARY POWER OTHER THAN DETERRENCE

Defense officials justify U.S. military buildup as a deterrent—to preserve the peace through strength. Looking more closely, however, we discover that our expanding arsenal is meant to serve certain other purposes. As Jonathan Schell has observed, these are "less frequently voiced" and "less defensible."[29]

We begin to suspect this when we realize that the United States has more than 10,000 strategic nuclear warheads, approximately half of which are deployed on submarines, invulnerable to a Soviet first strike.[30] Jerome Wiesner, former president of Massachusetts Institute of Technology and science adviser to Presidents Eisenhower and Kennedy, is one of many informed individuals who estimate that 400 to 900 warheads would be more than enough to destroy all major Soviet cities and military installations, even after riding out a surprise attack.[31]

1. To support foreign policy. Why the tremendous surplus? Members of the defense establishment itself, in less guarded moments, supply some of the answers. Note the reason Kenneth Adelman, who was to become director of the U.S. Arms Control and Disarmament Agency, in 1981 called for better offensive weapons, including new ground-based missiles, strategic bombers, and nuclear submarines: "U.S. strategic forces do not exist solely to deter a Soviet nuclear attack. . . . Rather, they are intended to support a range of U.S. foreign policy goals."[32] President Carter specified one of these goals in warning that the United States would go to war, if necessary, to protect its "vital interests" in the Persian Gulf region.[33] With bases, naval power, and alliances backed up by nuclear weapons, the United States strives for political domination in many parts of the globe. The Soviet Union does the same thing insofar as it is able.

Pursuing foreign policy objectives, the United States has threatened at least twelve times to use nuclear weapons. For example, in 1953, President Eisenhower threatened to use atomic bombs against China and North Korea to force a settlement of the Korean War. In his memoirs, Eisenhower confided: "In the Formosa Straits area . . . we dropped the word, discreetly, of our intention. We felt quite sure it would reach Soviet and Chinese Communist ears."[34]

Less explicit threats have been implied by sending nuclear bombers and ships to troubled areas. A case in point was Truman's deployment in 1948 of "atomic-capable" B-29s to bases in Britain and Germany to break the blockade of Berlin by intimidating the Soviet Union.[35]

In addition to threats, there have been several ominous cases when U.S. officials, including Presidents Eisenhower and Nixon, have secretly planned to use nuclear weapons. In 1954, Secretary of State John Foster Dulles twice offered to Prime Minister Georges Bidault of France the use of atomic weapons—first against Communist China and later against the Vietminh forces at Dien Bien Phu. Bidault had the sense to decline both offers. In respect to the first, he pointed out that it "would be impossible to predict where the use of nuclear weapons against Red China would end, that it could lead to Russian intervention and a world-wide holocaust."[36]

Nearly all the threats and offers have been directed against small nations that had ties to the Soviet Union but did not possess the bomb, or against the Soviet Union before it had the means to retaliate. Now that the Soviets have achieved parity with the United States, overt threats have decreased. Because the earlier threats were often effective, however, U.S. policymakers tend to continue the "tough guy" approach. Therein may lie our doom, for the policymakers fail to take account of the Soviet resolve after the Cuban missile crisis. This was expressed by V. Kuznetsov, the Soviet negotiator of the missile withdrawal. Talking with the American negotiator, John J. McCloy, at the latter's home, Kuznetsov warned, "You Americans will never be able to do this to us again."[37]

When the United States has threatened a nonnuclear state or the Soviet Union, or when the threat was only in the minds of the planners, the weapons were obviously not being used as deterrents. And when the United States relies on its nuclear striking power to make commitments in many parts of

16

the world—often to unstable states that could easily involve the United States in their hostilities—its strength makes war more likely, rather than less. This is scarcely what a deterrent is supposed to do.

In maintaining global spheres of influence, U.S. planners are willing to risk nuclear war, and hence the destruction of the nation. Jonathan Schell has expressed this contradiction aptly:

> While the aim of survival causes statesmen to declare regularly that no purpose could ever be served by a holocaust, and that the aim of nuclear policy can only be to prevent such insanity, the pursuit of national objectives forces them to declare in the next breath that they are unwaveringly resolved to perpetrate exactly this unjustifiable and insane action if some nation threatens a "vital interest" of theirs.[38]

It is abundantly clear that the purpose of nuclear arsenals is not only to deter enemy attacks, but also to impose our will on other nations.

2. *To fight and win wars.* Many sensitive individuals who recognize the immorality of using nuclear weapons do not object to them, because they assume that they are only deterrents and will not actually be used. This assumption is now refuted by the military leaders themselves, however, who refer openly to the twofold functions of the weapons—to deter war and to prevail if deterrence fails.[39] Unfortunately, these two functions are contradictory. Creating the means to fight a war increases the probability of getting into it, rather than deterring it.

Without admitting it publicly, or perhaps even to themselves, advocates of "peace through strength" seem to recognize that this is more a slogan than a realistic policy. Hence they assure us that nuclear war will not be so bad after all—that it would be survivable. They advocate civil defense, hospital contingency plans, and antiballistic missile systems. The tremendous overkill capacity that the United States is increasing daily, superfluous for deterrence, can be justified only in terms of fighting a war.

It has long been recognized that the United States is prepared to use nuclear weapons first if war breaks out in Europe or in the Persian Gulf area. This is considered necessary to counter a Soviet attack with allegedly superior conventional forces. It is less well known that in recent years, U.S. strategy has increasingly emphasized the capacity to begin a war by a nuclear first strike on the Soviet homeland. Directive 59, issued by President Carter, provides for counterforce strategy—targeting Soviet missile silos and command centers. Modified Minuteman III, MX, Trident D-5, and Pershing II missiles now have the accuracy and hard-target kill capability to destroy steel-and-concrete-reinforced silos. They have the velocity to implement a surprise attack. The MX and Pershing II missiles are vulnerable to Soviet attack; they are useful only if they strike before being struck.

Jack Anderson, Washington columnist for United Feature Syndicate, has obtained secret reports of the Defense Department and the Arms Control and Disarmament Agency that are quite revealing. These reports predict that by 1993, the United States will be able to knock out practically every Soviet missile silo. Most of the U.S. missiles satisfy first-strike requirements in being able drastically to impair the Soviet ability to retaliate.[40]

U.S. Presidents assert that U.S. weapons are solely for defense. But a realistic appraisal must pay more attention to capabilities than to official statements. Military aggressors usually claim to be acting defensively. American cluster bombs were sold to Israel on condition that they were to be used only in response to attack, but Israel used them in the invasion of Lebanon in 1982. The line between offense and defense is not always clear. A good offense may be considered the best defense. Even before Directive 59, Lieutenant General Bernard A. Schriever, then Commander, U.S. Air Research and Development Command, proclaimed: "The only adequate deterrent strength would . . . enable this country, if it chose, to strike the first blow and wipe out Russia." In a thorough study published in 1985, Daniel Ford cites numerous U.S. military planners who are determined, to quote an Air Force strategist, that "if there is a nuclear war the United States will be the one to start it."[41]

In addition to nuclear weapons especially suited for a first strike are those intended for conducting a nuclear war. The neutron bomb, which has no deterrent function, is a case in point. The role of deterrence doctrine in rationalizing prolonged warfighting is revealed in an Air Force basic combat manual, rewritten in 1984. It argues: "The medium of space provides an unlimited potential and opportunity for military operations on which the Air Force must capitalize. . . . The nation's highest defense priority—deterrence—requires a credible warfighting capability across the spectrum of conflict."[42]

If U.S defense strategists were primarily interested in deterrence, they would also be primarily concerned with ending a nuclear war once it has started. But in the article "Victory Is Possible," Colin Gray and Keith Payne leave no doubt that they consider "the determination to wage nuclear war at ever higher levels of violence" and the "demise of the Soviet state" more important than bringing the slaughter to the earliest possible end.[43] Reports of the Pentagon scenario for a protracted nuclear war, and of statements by Defense Secretary Weinberger, Navy Secretary John Lehman, Vice-President George Bush, and several other top-level defense officials, reveal plans to continue the war until the United States prevails.[44]

Although defense analysts assign varying meanings to the word prevail, several envisage not merely unconditional surrender, but "annihilating the Soviet political-military leadership . . . while simultaneously destroying the urban-industrial heartland of the U.S.S.R."[45] Only then will they be willing to end the war. Their firm priority to prevail is chilling, to put it mildly. Perhaps in answer to criticism of this emphasis, Secretary Weinberger has asserted that our aim would be

19

to "restore peace." Note, however, the conditions he added: The war must be ended "on favorable terms. . . . We must defeat the attack and achieve our national objectives while limiting—to the extent possible and practicable—the scope of the conflict."[46] Taking into account all the available evidence and the doublespeak of the war planners, we must conclude that there has been no basic change of policy.

Although the chance of a nuclear war between the United States and the Soviet Union is great, the chance of its being conducted on a low enough level to last very long is not. But if it were somehow protracted, it could, at any moment, become an all-out holocaust that would destroy both sides, as well as noncombatant nations. Therefore, the preeminent goal should be to end it. To insist on prevailing could magnify the slaughter manyfold. It might even make the difference between some sort of recovery and the end of all human life.

Although quite horrifying, it is not surprising that nuclear weapons have roles other than as deterrents. The military strategists are simply following the tradition of their profession; their function is not to prevent wars, but to fight and win them. This means building as large an arsenal as possible and planning to use it. B.T. Feld, editor of *The Bulletin of the Atomic Scientists*, puts it bluntly:

> *The military technologists have never been willing to accept the relegation of nuclear weapons to a purely deterrent role; they have continued to develop . . . weapons technology in ways that might lead to the acceptability of nuclear weapons into the ordinary arsenals of conventional "war fighting." . . . And they have pressed inexorably for the acceptance by society of the concept of "tactical or limited" nuclear war.*[47]

In his perceptive volume, *Brighter Than a Thousand Suns*, Robert Jungk reports that during World War II, government officials persuaded scientists in the United States to work on the atom bomb on the grounds "that there was no intention of using the new bomb in warfare. It was merely to serve as a deterrent in case the Germans developed a similar

20

weapon. . . . Their work would be contributing to the preservation of the whole nation from a catastrophe."[48]

In private, a major attached to the War Department shocked Samuel Goudsmit, a Dutch nuclear physicist working on the American bomb project, with the prophecy: "If we have such a weapon, we are going to use it."[49] We are all affected by the psychological truth that when we develop a mechanism for a certain purpose, we have a strong desire to see it work. After Germany surrendered, did General Leslie Groves halt the atom bomb project, of which he had charge? Definitely not! Instead, he "gave the impression of being obsessed by one intense fear, that the war [with Japan] would be finished before his bomb could be."[50]

Similar instances indicate that pursuing peace through the apparatus of war gives too much power to the military in shaping foreign policy. During the missile crisis of 1962, the Joint Chiefs of Staff kept pressing for air strikes against Cuba that could have precipitated a nuclear war, rather than advocating a diplomatic solution aimed at avoiding it.[51]

Building up ever more devastating weapons systems is rationalized in the name of deterrence, but it creates a juggernaut that roars ever faster in the wrong direction, overriding all efforts to control or reverse it. The momentum of the German and Russian military machines helped to precipitate World War I. This is relevant to the present-day claim that the United States is increasing its arsenal as a bargaining chip to reduce it. Efforts at deterrence through escalating U.S. arsenals and efforts at arms reduction are mutually contradictory. The whole set of processes that make up an allegedly deterrent fighting machine, from the scientific laboratory to the field of battle, takes on a life of its own and develops a momentum that leads to war.

SOME MISCONCEPTIONS

1. That military weakness invites attack. Proponents of deterrence through strength sometimes argue that military weakness encourages a potential enemy to launch an attack. This statement contains a grain of truth. Unprovoked aggression by a strong nation against a weaker one may occur. But strong nations often attack each other. The circumstances in which wars begin are so varied that one can only speculate whether strength or weakness is more likely to be attacked. The historical record is inconclusive. But pertinent observations are in order.

Often one nation attacks another for reasons so compelling or fortuitous that it scarcely regards the military strength of the opponent. Sometimes a nation attacks another precisely because the other is so strong, or is expected to become so strong, that the attacker wants the advantage of a first strike. A cold war mentality produces fear and hostility such that nation *A* may be tempted to strike nation *B* when the latter is temporarily weaker. But the basic incentive is not the weakness of nation *B*. The real cause is the arms race, generating fear of the strength that *B* had before and will presumably have again. A peaceful nation with no menacing arsenal would elicit no such reaction.

Periodically, U.S. Presidents point with alarm to alleged weapons gaps, implying weakness relative to the Soviet Union. Their purpose is to persuade Congress and the public that a larger war budget is needed. If they really believed that the United States was so vulnerable, they would not advertise it. If the Soviets really thought the United States was so weak, and if weakness invites aggression, why have they not launched an attack?

To provide the security nuclear weapons are supposed to give, a nation does not need more megatonnage than its rival, and it is no disadvantage to have less. It needs only enough to destroy the other. Nuclear weapons are so destructive that unacceptable damage can be inflicted without directly attacking the enemy's armed forces and in spite of the greater firepower the opponent may have. The comparative military strength of the United States and the Soviet Union is irrelevant because each has enough nuclear weapons to obliterate the other innumerable times. Either side could reduce its arsenal independently of the other with no risk.

In comparing the risks involved in reducing arsenals with those involved in expanding them, an additional factor must be considered in the nuclear age. The danger is not just of a deliberate attack by the other side, but of getting into war, regardless of which side starts it and whether it is deliberate or accidental. In the past, the danger was that of losing. Now the danger is that of war breaking out, since both sides would lose. This means that a nation needs to fear itself as well as its rivals because a heavily armed nation is more likely than a weaker one to precipitate a war by engaging in brinkmanship and provocative acts.

The hatred and fear generated by deterrence strategy, plus the hair-trigger weapons being developed, have created such an explosive situation that almost any action involves some risk. Everything considered, however, military strength is probably more likely to lead to war than is so-called weakness. The risk is less for the nation that is less militaristic. It may well be that "the meek shall inherit the earth."

2. That deterrence is considered merely a temporary strategy. Some of those who advocate military might as a deterrent sense that it would be unsatisfactory as a permanent policy. Hence they contend that it is only meant to be temporary—until arms reduction makes it no longer necessary. Some add that the weapons are simply to serve as short-term bargaining chips. During the four decades of the so-called nuclear deterrent, however, the United States has made no progress toward phasing out the weapons. It has increased their number far beyond any possible deterrent or defensive functions. They have caused the present situation to be so much more dangerous that we cannot wait much longer.

More to the point: There is little reason to suppose that U.S. policymakers really intend to dismantle any weapons, except those that become obsolete, are clearly superfluous, or are replaced by more effective ones. Before the peace movement caused him to change his rhetoric, President Reagan made this quite clear when he declared to a West Point audience: "The argument . . . will be over which weapons [to build], not whether we should forsake weaponry for treaties and agreements."[52] A careful reading of official statements from the Department of Defense and the State Department echoes this intention, albeit not always so bluntly.[53] It is scarcely realistic to conceive of the government spending billions of dollars on such systems as MX missiles—only to destroy them soon after.

3. *That deterrence works.* A frequently heard rationale for U.S. foreign policy in general and deterrence in particular is that it has succeeded in preventing nuclear war. This has been claimed innumerable times by Caspar Weinberger and other proponents of peace through strength. In the words of President Reagan: "The policy of deterrence has stood the test of time. . . . It has worked for nearly forty years."[54]

This is usually asserted as if it were obvious, not subject to question. Indeed, it seems plausible—until we examine it more closely with special reference to the assumptions behind it. Two questions need to be raised. The first is whether the net effect of U.S. deterrence policy has, in fact, been to reduce the likelihood of nuclear war. The second is whether it can be expected to do so in the future. Neither question can be answered with finality. The best we can do is to take into account as many relevant factors as possible and then draw the most reasonable conclusions.

Despite U.S. nuclear arsenals, many conventional wars have occurred, including those in Korea and Vietnam that involved the United States. As indicated earlier, a nuclear threat probably has some deterrent effect. It may have helped to prevent the spread of local conflicts. But no solid basis exists for the common assumption that ever since World War II, the Soviet Union has had a compelling urge to attack Western Europe or the United States, and that only the U.S. nuclear deterrent has kept them at bay. In their exhaustive, prize-winning volume, *Deterrence in American Foreign Policy: Theory and Practice,* Stanford University scholars Alexander L. George and Richard Smoke expressed this conclusion: "A major power which takes on the role of protector of allies, as the United States has done, may frequently be deterring a threat which does not exist. . . . The absence of attack could mean either that no attack was ever intended or that deterrence has succeeded."[55]

In view of the dangers attendant on the arms race that the deterrence buildup intensifies, the United States has avoided nuclear war not because of the deterrence of its military strength, but despite the provocative effect of that strength. In any case, we should not accept without question the simplistic assertions of U.S. policymakers.

The second question is more crucial: whether current U.S. foreign policy, based on peace through strength, can be expected to prevent nuclear war in the future. No matter how one views the past, an objective consideration of four recent developments leads to the conclusion that ominous changes are occurring. What seems to have "worked" before may not do so under different conditions. As a consequence, large-scale nuclear war is virtually certain to erupt unless the United States drastically alters its policy.

The first development consists of the dynamic progress in weapons technology. Obviously, the danger increases as both superpowers deploy additional nuclear weapons. More serious are the continuous "improvements" being made in the weapons and the development of new weapons. The creation of smaller, faster, more accurate missiles and of stealth bombers and other radar-defying delivery systems, although done ostensibly for deterrence, clearly has the opposite effect. It keeps upsetting the balance of terror, which was unstable in the first place.

The chances of serious accidents, miscalculations, launch-on-warning, and a preemptive first strike, especially in a crisis, increase as time goes on. Sydney Drell, deputy director of the Linear Accelerator Center of Stanford University, has rightly observed: "Rapidly advancing weapons technology and the growing repertoire of uses for nuclear weapons are threatening to remove even the limited security we have sought through mutual deterrence."[56]

A second cause of our increasing danger is the rejection of détente and the renewal of the cold war, evidenced by the more bellicose attitude of our national leaders. President Reagan's reference to the Soviets as liars and cheats, his labeling the Soviet Union as the "focus of evil," and his "joke" about bombing in five minutes hardly foster peaceful relations. Consider also the implications of the President's speech at the U.N. Second Special Session on Disarmament in June 1982. He could have created an atmosphere conducive to the flexibility each side must have in order to reach the accords needed to avert war. Instead, he delivered a highly biased, vitriolic attack on the Soviet Union and a self-righteous recital of the alleged virtues of U.S. foreign policy. Such an utterance only begets an equally belligerent response.

If we are to have enduring peace, we must learn to get along with the Soviets. They are hard enough to live with; we need not exacerbate the sore! Like other side effects of deterrence strategy, fomenting hatred makes war more likely. (On occasion, policymakers use more conciliatory rhetoric, but this is not matched by action, and the Soviets cannot be expected to forget the more spontaneous utterances.)

A third factor that makes our situation ever more perilous is the increasing emphasis, noted earlier, on fighting and winning a protracted nuclear war.

The fourth process is the proliferation mentioned earlier. In the course of time, more fingers become poised above the nuclear button. As B.T. Feld, writing in his capacity as secretary-general of the Pugwash Council on Science and World Affairs, has pointed out, our "deterrence, whatever its successes in the past, is inherently unstable and unworkable in the increasingly multipolar world."[57] A State Department specialist confirmed this when he declared that if they had them, Iran and Iraq would probably use nuclear weapons in their conflict.[58] A former foreign policy analyst for the State Department, Richard Barnet, summarizes the increasing danger:

> *The list of potential flashpoints for nuclear war is a long one. . . . And the materials and technology for creating nuclear weapons are ever more widely available. These developments greatly increase the likelihood of new U.S.- Soviet confrontations. . . . We cannot always count on the Soviets to back down; their remarkable record of restraint in a crisis . . . is a reflection of their relative military weakness in the past.*
>
> *Having achieved rough parity with the United States in military power, their national security managers are now much more likely to think like their U.S. counterparts: "We can't afford to back down and be exposed as a pitiful, helpless giant." Thus the happy accident that the world has survived the first . . . years of the nuclear era is unimpressive evidence that we can avoid nuclear war in the coming era, for world power relationships are changing faster than we can comprehend, and the arms race has become an entirely new game.*[59]

In assessing the future, we need to be aware not only of the four developments just outlined, but also of the lessons of history and the law of probabilities. The peace we are experiencing now resembles the peace that preceded World War I and innumerable past wars. Deterrence (peace through strength) has certainly failed more often than it has succeeded. As Major General Maurice stated after World War I, "I went into the British army believing that if you want peace, you must prepare for war. I believe now that if you prepare for war you will get war."

Granted, the longer we remain at peace, the more complacent we may become, and the more it may appear that deterrence is effective. The only definitive proof to the contrary would be the actual outbreak of war. Then it would be too late. The situation is like that of reckless drivers. The longer they manage to avoid an accident, the more confident and reckless they become. They may even attribute their safety to their method of driving. They will be convinced otherwise only after they have an accident.

We have been lucky to escape the holocaust so far, despite accidents, miscalculations, and brinkmanship. But four decades is a short time. How long can we continue on the road of infinite military expansion, rationalized by the theory of deterrence? To suppose that the United States can avoid nuclear war much longer while continuing its present foreign policy is like tossing a coin repeatedly and expecting it always to come up heads.

This is convincingly demonstrated by Bradford Lyttle in his perceptive essay, *The Flaw in Deterrence*. Analyzing the writings of several influential deterrence strategists, Lyttle shows that they almost invariably overlook the implications of mathematical probability theory. They fail to realize that the risk of war by way of military deterrence becomes greater in proportion to the time span being considered. For example, although the likelihood of accidental war under present conditions may not be great on one particular day, it becomes practically certain in a time span of several years.[60] Analyses of the relevant data by statisticians confirm Lyttle's conclusions.[61] As Jonathan Schell has stated, "Unless we rid ourselves of our nuclear arsenals a holocaust not only *might* occur but *will* occur—if not today, then tomorrow; if not this year, then the next."[62] In this connection, we must remember that for the first time in history a single error could destroy us all.

Although it will not be easy, we can reverse the present trend. But we must not evade the task by what Inga Thorsson, the Swedish undersecretary of state, has called "an erroneous perception of safety."[63]

CONCLUSION

I have attempted to show that the U.S. stated policy of deterring war by increasing military strength is illusory.

Moreover, the United States is escalating its military capability not only to deter an attack, but also to wield a big stick in support of its foreign policy and to prepare for fighting a nuclear war. John Hersey, the author of *Hiroshima*, summarizes our self-deception:

> The central moral crime against the future of the human race is the use being made by superpowers of the idea of deterrence. . . . It is a potentially murderous lie. "Deterrence" causes an endless escalation of provocations, which are bound to lead one day to war. . . . The moment one side develops a new, irresistible, more accurate weapon, the other side must in the name of deterrence counter by producing another even more invulnerable and devastating system. This has reached a point . . . of an insane equation of "deterrence" with the capability of winning a protracted nuclear war.[64]

Only by reversing the arms race and adopting a radically different foreign policy can the United States attain true security.

Chapter II.

REDUCING
THE SOVIET THREAT

THE DOCTRINE OF deterrence implies the existence of a military threat that needs to be deterred. This leads us directly to the main source of such a threat—the Soviet Union.

What about the Russians? No question is raised more frequently in discussions about world peace. Many an otherwise good idea is shot down because it fails to deal adequately with the alleged "Soviet Threat." Just what is this threat? How serious is it? What do leading specialists on the Soviet Union say about it? This chapter attempts to answer these questions. Chapter I shows that the deployment of nuclear weapons only makes the threat worse. A later chapter focuses on better ways to cope with the problem.

I address this topic not as an expert in Soviet affairs, but as one who has studied the experts and tried to apply common sense and clear thinking to the issues. Because several good books and pamphlets have examined the subject (see Bibliography), my treatment of it is relatively brief.

The fear of the Soviets is based on their military power and their willingness to use it or to threaten its use. In this way, they have kept a tight grip on their Eastern European satellites—particularly Hungary, Czechoslovakia, and Poland—and tried to maintain control in Afghanistan. Through military aid and the use of Cuban proxy forces, they have extended their reach into Angola, Ethiopia, and other Third

World nations. The Soviet influence in Central America, notably Cuba and Nicaragua, brings the threat closer to home.

Especially disquieting is the U.S. conception of the Soviet ideology as envisaging world domination through military power. If this fear is based on reality, it would appear that we must be forever vigilant, since the United States would be the major victim in the relentless Soviet pursuit of this goal. Our anxiety is compounded by the repressive nature of the Soviet regime—the violations of human rights as evidenced in the harsh treatment of dissidents. When we ask ourselves just how the Soviet Union threatens the United States, we find that most of our fears are vague and difficult to pin down. Quite a gap exists between our anxiety and what could actually occur. In worst-case scenarios, however, we can imagine three ways that we are threatened.

THREE TYPES OF THREAT

1. To conquer Western Europe and the United States. Probably our most pervasive fear is that the Soviets would conquer Western European countries, install their rulers or puppets there, and then invade the United States. We picture Soviet conquerors actually governing our nation—suppressing our freedom and forcing atheistic communism on us. The more we think about this in concrete terms, the more we realize how unlikely a scenario it is. The Soviets have great difficulty controlling the countries within their sphere of influence. Poland is the most conspicuous case, while East Germany, Hungary, and Czechoslovakia, for example, have added to the problems of the Kremlin in maintaining its control.

A leading authority on Warsaw Pact countries is Gordon Skilling, political science professor at the University of Toronto. In a University of Michigan Briefing on Soviet Affairs, he demonstrated in considerable detail that the Soviet bloc in Eastern Europe is in a constant state of crisis that has burst into a major upheaval every twelve years.[1] He pointed

31

out that in trying to deal with its European satellites, the Soviet Union is faced with an insoluble contradiction in policy. To avoid upheavals by keeping the people happy, it needs to allow greater freedom and autonomy. But it insists on uniformity, for the sake of which it resorts to coercion and repression.

As the Eastern bloc countries face the future, the only certainty Skilling sees for them is a continuation of chronic crisis, creating insoluble problems for the Soviet Union. A special problem noted by Brian May, *Manchester Guardian* analyst, is that a successful conquest of Europe would probably lead to a united armed Germany.[2] Even under Soviet control, this is the last thing the Kremlin would want. Under these circumstances, it is unrealistic to conceive of the Soviet Union compounding its difficulties by trying to add West Germany and other European nations to its empire. It has much more to gain by maintaining and expanding economic relations with them. Pointing out that pressures for political reform in Eastern Europe threaten to spread to the Soviet Union itself, the high-level Alternative Defence Commission in Britain summarizes the situation:

> *It is clear that a Soviet attack upon and military occupation of one or several West European countries would increase its military and administrative burdens, probably add to its political problems in controlling satellite states, and result in a disruption of relations with Western Europe, or . . . in the destruction of the existing West European economy, all of which would exacerbate economic and political problems inside the USSR and Eastern Europe.[3]*

Presumably the Soviet Union would not seek to conquer the United States until it had occupied Europe. The difficulties it has in controlling its current satellites and the greater burdens it would have in Western Europe would be dwarfed by the problems incurred in seeking to invade and govern the United States. In fact, these problems would be insurmountable, whether or not Western Europe had previously been occupied. Studies by the chief authority on the subject, Michael Klare, fellow of the Institute for Policy Studies, show that the Soviet Union "does not possess a capacity for long range intervention against well-equipped adversaries."[4] And it stretches the imagination to conceive of a foreign dictator subduing the American people!

To be sure, as Barbara Tuchman points out in *The March of Folly,* nations do not always act rationally to promote their interests.[5] The belief is widespread that the Soviets are driven by their ideology to seek military conquest of the world. Actually, neither official doctrine nor Soviet behavior provides a basis for this view. A foremost specialist on Soviet foreign policy, Fred Warner Neal, professor of government at the Claremont Graduate School, notes:

> *No matter how much hostility for capitalism was implicit in all this ideology, there was nothing calling for initiation of military action by Moscow. To make up for this lack, there has arisen a body of wholly false quotations attributed to Lenin, Stalin, and others, in which they carefully explained that all the Russians were waiting for was for the West to let down its guard.[6]*

Marxist-Leninist doctrine does call for worldwide communism. But this is to be achieved by internal revolutions, rather than by Soviet military aggression. Capitalism is considered so inherently defective that it is doomed to collapse, whereas the Soviet system is destined to prevail because of its intrinsic worth: the correlation of forces is in its favor. In recent decades, this has increasingly been anticipated as coming gradually, as the superiority of communism becomes evident, rather than by violent upheavals. Krushchev's famous outburst, "We will bury you," is interpreted this way by Arkady Shevchenko, a high Soviet official who was present on the occasion.[7] Khrushchev's prediction that Eisenhower's grandchildren would be Communists reflected this same expectation.

The course of history has not borne out such predictions.

Joseph F. Nye Jr., professor of government at Harvard University, points out that "Khrushchev's 1959 claims to overtake and bury the United States have turned out to be hollow boasts."[8] The worldwide spread of communism has failed to occur. Many scholars believe that, on balance, the influence of the Soviet Union beyond its borders has been declining. In a survey of Soviet gains and losses around the world from 1945 to 1980, the *Defense Monitor* of the Center for Defense Information concludes, "Soviet setbacks in China, Indonesia, Egypt, India, and Iraq dwarf marginal advances in lesser countries."[9]

As a consequence, the orthodox ideology of attaining worldwide hegemony seems to many to be losing its hold on Soviet officials, especially members of the younger generation. But Paul H. Nitze, U.S. special representative for arms control negotiations, questions this view. He writes: "Marxist-Leninist ideology . . . continues to have an important influence on Soviet policymaking. . . . Compromise on the dogma would be suicidal for the regime. . . . It is the linchpin of the system."[10] Perhaps the most accurate assessment is that of Alexander Dallin, a specialist in modern Russian history. He suggests that while Soviet officials often give lip service to the traditional ideology, it no longer has a significant effect on their decisions and conduct.[11]

Among competent analysts who share Dallin's view are Harvard historian Edward Keenan; Marshall D. Shulman, professor of international relations at Columbia University; Alfred Meyer, professor of political science at the University of Michigan; John Bennett, authority on ethical aspects of foreign policy; Yugoslavia's Milovan Djilas; former Ambassador Walter T. Stoessel; and foreign correspondents Hedrick Smith and Robert Kaiser.[12] In similar vein, Sovietologist Dimitri Simes, of the Carnegie Endowment for International Peace, contends that the Soviet Union can best be understood today as a typical great nation competing for power and influence in the world. Its approach is pragmatic rather than ideological; it seizes whatever opportunities arise to pursue its national interests. In so doing, it has been cautious and prudent rather than revolutionary. "The days of the Communist International are over," declares Simes.[13]

From this perspective, the Soviet involvement in Afghanistan and its determined effort to maintain control of its Eastern European satellites are not seen as evidence of a master plan for world domination. They reflect, rather, a desire for buffer states to protect the nation from potential aggressors. The Soviets have three reasons for seeing this as a very real need: They lack the protection afforded by geographical boundaries, such as large bodies of water; they have suffered many invasions over the years; and they are virtually encircled by hostile powers.

2. To destroy the United States. It seems evident that Soviet intentions and behavior are best explained in terms of big-power rivalry beyond its borders and perceived defense needs closer to home, rather than in terms of seeking to conquer Western Europe or the United States. Nevertheless, two real threats to the United States must be recognized. The first is that with a massive arsenal of intercontinental ballistic missiles able to reach U.S. shores in thirty minutes, the Soviet Union now poses a direct threat that was impossible before the nuclear era. The threat is to bomb us into oblivion. Pentagon officials use this to justify escalation of U.S. arsenals.

Each of the superpowers is now able to destroy the other, and each multiplies its warheads in order to counter the other. This only compounds the danger. When we ask what motive the Soviet Union could have for obliterating the United States, we can conceive of only one answer. It could not be to seize U.S. resources, for they would be destroyed. The only possible motive would be the Soviets' fear of U.S. nuclear bombs aimed at them and the advantage they would gain by striking first. Moreover, if the United States were not menacing them, a nuclear attack on us would be condemned by the whole civilized world, whereas a U.S. threat to them could justify their launching a preemptive strike in self-defense. In these and other respects, the "strength" that is supposed to protect us creates the very threat that we fear.

Remember that the United States, not the Soviet Union, is chiefly responsible for the arms race. We initiated practically every new step in the upward spiral. As Thomas Powers, Pulitzer Prize winner and author of *Thinking About the Next War*, has pointed out:

> *The Americans were first with the bomb, first with a workable thermonuclear weapon, first with the long-range bomber, first with an effective intercontinental-missile fleet, first with hardened missile silos, first with missile-firing submarines, first with multiple warheads that could be independently targeted. Every new system increased the danger.*[14]

We called these systems purely defensive. But the Soviets perceived them as threats. They felt impelled to make the economic sacrifices necessary to match them with similar "deterrents," which we perceive as threats. The sad truth is that we could have decreased the danger at any time by foregoing the opportunity to develop new weapons systems.

Concerning the likelihood of a direct Soviet attack, two conclusions may now be drawn: First, a careful examination of the Soviets' actions and their situation in the world does not support the view that they would attack us if we did not threaten them with our so-called deterrent. Second, insofar as a real threat exists, it can only be reduced, and eventually eliminated, by abolishing the weapons that constitute the threat.

3. To encroach on U.S. vital interests. A third type of threat remains to be considered. It is that if Western Europe or the United States were much weaker militarily than the Soviet Union, it would be subject to blackmail. Our affluent life-style could be endangered by Soviet encroachments on our vital interests. This is a more realistic fear, since it represents a genuine possibility. I shall discuss it more fully in chapter V.

Meanwhile, we may gain perspective by considering the possible fate of a nation subject to "Finlandization." This term is used by those who recognize that there is no real danger of a Soviet invasion of Western Europe, but who see Finland as an unfortunate example of a nation that is subservient to the Soviet Union. It is instructive to note that even though the Soviet Union defeated Finland in war, it has not attempted to govern it. To some extent, Finland must defer to its more powerful neighbor, but its citizens would not "rather be dead."

Many nations are subservient to or dependent on others, as are Canada and Mexico to the United States. Yet they do not consider this an intolerable handicap. In his study of Soviet foreign policy, Jonathan Steele, chief foreign correspondent for *The Guardian*, contends that the Kremlin's influence on Finland "has been minimal"—no greater than that exerted by the Ford Administration on France and Italy when it warned them against including Communists in their governments. He concludes, "The concept of Finlandization is an empty myth."[15]

The people of Finland are better off than they would be if their country were a heavily armed threat to, and hence a target of, the Soviet Union. Certainly the threat of Finlandization is not serious enough to warrant risking nuclear war. This is the key issue. The time is past when the United States could dominate the world without serious competition. It is better to be content with a lesser role than to risk the moral atrocity of slaughtering millions of Soviet civilians and being slaughtered in return.

WHY THE UNITED STATES MAGNIFIES THE THREAT

Up to this point, I have contended that the most serious threat is the one the United States has created by menacing the Soviet Union. One might ask why we magnify our threat by continually deploying new missiles, thereby provoking a response that adds to our jeopardy. It doesn't appear to make sense—for the simple reason that it doesn't make sense in terms of survival. In chapter I, I examined two reasons, other than deterrence, for increasing the U.S. stockpile of nuclear weapons: to support an aggressive foreign policy and to develop a warfighting capability. An additional reason is so obvious that it can be dealt with quickly.

1. To serve vested interests. Such giant corporations as General Electric receive billions of dollars a year in war business. With an eye to short-term gain, rather than the longer-term welfare of themselves or society, business executives expend large sums and great effort to keep Pentagon contracts rolling in. Union leaders and employees welcome the jobs thus provided (although the same money spent other ways would create more jobs). Legislators pass appropriation bills to support war industries in their districts. The late Senator Henry Jackson, a leading advocate of increased military spending, was rightly called "the Senator from Boeing," a company with annual war contracts totaling billions of dollars. No wonder Boeing contributed heavily to his 1976 presidential bid!

Community leaders, of course, find it popular to applaud local defense spending. University professors want funding for research. Each branch of the armed forces naturally seeks to expand its own program by pressing for more weapons. The President is eager to satisfy such desires and to project American power abroad. Because none of these benefits would survive a nuclear war, they are illusory. But when jobs, financial security, prestige, and life-style appear to be at stake, it is easier to rationalize the status quo than to rock the boat.

The simplest and easiest rationale for all this is to point to the alleged Soviet menace. As Senator Arthur Vandenberg advised President Truman, if the government intended to increase military spending, it would have to "scare the hell out of the country."[16] Alan Wolfe points out in *The Rise and Fall of*

38

the Soviet Threat that the degree of emphasis on the threat is determined more by political factors in the United States than by actions of the Soviet Union. As an example, he cites a cable sent to Washington in 1948 by General Lucius Clay, commander of American forces in West Germany. The cable greatly exaggerated Soviet hostility during negotiations over Berlin, giving the impression that war might be in the offing. Later he admitted that the primary purpose of the cable was to assist the military chiefs in their congressional testimony. It was not related to any change in Soviet strategy.[17]

Referring to "terrifying exaggerations of military danger," Jerome Wiesner writes: "During every presidential election campaign, we are subjected to a bombardment of hysterical, frightening estimates of impending Soviet strategic superiority, accompanied by calls for a major buildup of our nuclear forces."[18] As we implement the buildup and the Soviets follow suit, the threat becomes greater, making the scare tactics more credible.

2. To provide a scapegoat. A further reason we fall victims to anti-Soviet rhetoric is that it fills a psychological need. The United States has long taken for granted its position as the most powerful nation in the world. It has used its power to dominate other nations politically, economically, and militarily. But Germany and Japan, with lesser military burdens, have become economic rivals, and Third World nations are becoming forces to reckon with more seriously. The United States grows uneasy as they assert themselves in the United Nations and the World Court. The oil-producing nations have demonstrated that the United States cannot push them around. The Islamic world is claiming its right to recognition.

We are not to blame for this erosion of U.S. dominance. It is simply part of the historical process. Yet we feel that somehow things have gone wrong; to assure ourselves that it is not our fault, we look for an enemy whom we can blame. The Soviet Union is the inevitable object of hostility, particularly because it has the effrontery to insist on being treated as an equal and tends to impede our Third World interventions. What better way to bolster our self-esteem than to tell ourselves that we are still Number One because our superior military might can meet the threat posed by the "enemy"?

PERCEPTIONS OF THE THREAT

To be sure, not everyone agrees with the assessment of the Soviet threat presented in this chapter. Members of the Committee on the Present Danger contend that only our capacity for massive nuclear retaliation has kept the Soviet Union from launching an attack. These include Professor Richard Pipes of Harvard University, Paul H. Nitze, Ronald Reagan, and some 30 more of the top 100 officials in the Reagan Administration.[19] In addition, a large segment of the general public has taken at face value the periodic cries of alarm to which it has been subjected. That is the reason for this chapter.

For the same reason, and to add credibility to my analyses, I note here a few of the many well-informed individuals—with no financial or political reasons to be biased—who have expressed the view that the Soviet Union has had no desire to wage war against Western Europe or the United States. In past decades, these have included John Foster Dulles, Robert A. Taft, Walter Lippman, James Forrestal, and General Douglas MacArthur.[20]

Typical of contemporary analysis is that of the eminent historian Henry Steele Commager: "We are threatened by a paranoia which sees the Soviet Union as a mortal enemy, bent on the destruction of the United States and of free nations everywhere. . . . There never has been . . . any basis for this fantasy."[21] Similar judgments have been made in recent years by Richard Barnet, former State Department analyst; James Blaker, former Secretary of Defense representative to the Mutual and Balanced Force Reduction (MBFR) talks in Vienna; Averell Harriman, former ambassador to the Soviet

Union; Michael Howard, distinguished British military historian; Gene R. La Rocque, Rear Admiral UNN (ret.); Robert Neild, professor of economics, Cambridge University; William Taubman, professor of political science, Amherst College; Jerome Wiesner; Senator J. William Fulbright.[22] Referring to the Soviet leaders, George Kennan writes: "I do not see them as men anxious to expand their power by the direct use of their armed forces, although they could easily be frightened into taking actions that would seem to have this aim. . . . I have seen no evidence that they are at all disposed to invade Western Europe."[23]

METHODS
OF REDUCING THE THREAT

My purpose to this point has been to assess the Soviet threat realistically. Obviously, the terrifying weapons of each side pose a threat to the other side. To reduce, and eventually eliminate, this threat, the United States must improve its relationship with the Soviet Union. Let me suggest certain attitudes and actions that should contribute to this end.

1. Facilitate informal high-level gatherings. The first Reagan-Gorbachev summit in November 1985 did not produce tangible results on arms control issues. Yet it did initiate a process of human interaction among top officials that should have positive long-term effects. Such events as the New Year greetings of the two leaders, the visits of Senator Edward Kennedy and other U.S. lawmakers with Gorbachev, and the conversations between the U.S. Secretary of State and the Soviet Foreign Minister provide opportunities for the policymakers of both sides to become acquainted with each other as human beings. This will help to overcome what George Kennan called "the dehumanization of any major national opponent, the tendency to form a . . . devil-image of that opponent, to deprive him in our imaginations of all normal human attributes."[24] We should encourage participants in such discussions to talk at length about the people of each country—how they view the other country, their aspirations, beliefs, fears, and prejudices. They should discuss the needs and problems of each nation, with plenty of chance to raise questions and clear up misunderstandings. The emphasis should be on listening to each other and being receptive to new ideas. This will expose U.S. leaders to the factors that cause aggressive Soviet behavior, such as the vulnerable situation of a nation encircled by hostile powers.

The atmosphere created by the summit may have been responsible for the omission from Reagan's State of the Union address several weeks later of derogatory references to the Soviet Union, such as accusations of treaty violations that he had repeated frequently before the meeting. To facilitate high-level conversations is essential because the success of negotiations may depend to a large extent on the feelings and perceptions of the negotiators.

2. *Facilitate wider mutual understanding and coopera-tion.* My next proposal is akin to the first. We should acceler-ate the development of a broad range of exchanges and joint projects involving not only policymakers, but also people from all ranks of life. In the early years of the Reagan Administra-tion, such contacts were curtailed. But at the first summit, Reagan and Gorbachev agreed on cooperative projects in environmental protection, fusion and cancer research, air safety, and educational exchanges. Progress is being made in some of these programs. In view of the budget-cutting efforts on both sides, however, vigilance is needed to maintain and expand them. Their significance goes beyond their stated objectives. They enable the participants from each nation to become acquainted with their counterparts on the other side. Peaceful relations between our two nations will be furthered in proportion as we heed the admonition of Kennan: "It is high time that we learned to see [the Soviet] people real-

istically, as the great body of normal human beings . . . strug-
gling with their modest personal problems . . . trying to bring
up children . . . to do the right thing . . . and to search like
ourselves for the meaning of life."[25]

3. *Recognize Soviet incentives for arms reduction.* More
accurate perceptions and better understanding should enable
us to follow my next suggestion: U.S. policymakers should
recognize the powerful incentives the Soviet Union has to
seek genuine arms reduction. Reagan Administration officials
repeatedly justified deploying intermediate-range missiles in
Europe on the ground that the Soviets lacked any incentive to
bargain seriously and that the deployment would induce them
to do so. It had exactly the opposite effect—causing them to
leave the bargaining table. Nevertheless, U.S. officials had the
effrontery to use the same argument in favor of installing MX
missiles.

The first incentive ignored by U.S. officials is the desire
to survive. The Soviets seem to have a greater awareness than
we do of how dangerous the arms race is. Second is the
difficulty they have keeping up with us in the competition that
depends so heavily on sophisticated technology in which we
are superior. To be able to reduce the pace would be for them
a tremendous relief. Third is their desperate need to alleviate
the burden placed by the military budget on their floundering
economy.[26] Fourth is the need to maintain internal political
stability. Several analysts agree that the governing bureaucrats
are experiencing increasing difficulty fulfilling the needs and
expectations of the population for consumer goods. To be able
to transfer funds from the military to the civilian sector would
be a real boon to them. Paul Warnke, arms negotiator during
the Carter Administration, confirms this: "In my negotiations,
I had the feeling that the Soviets were more serious than we
were—not because of any philanthropic impulses, not because
they're nice guys, but because they recognize that their political system is infinitely more fragile than ours."[27] With regard

to three of these incentives, we have common interests with the Soviets. We, too, would like to survive, to alleviate the burden on our economy, and to provide for human needs.

4. Take Soviet proposals seriously. In view of these incentives and the Soviet track record to date, we should take seriously the Soviet proposals for arms reduction. They have made many definite offers ever since Nikita Khrushchev's appeal at the U.N. session of 1959 for the total abolition of nuclear weapons.[28]

In 1973, the Soviets proposed a 10 percent reduction in the military budgets of the five permanent members of the U.N. Security Council, with 10 percent of the savings earmarked for economic assistance to developing countries.[29] Soviet Foreign Minister Andrei Gromyko later advocated a comprehensive test ban to be verified by on-site inspection. Several times the Soviets have made offers to halt or reduce the deployment of nuclear weapons in the European theater. These included a proposal for a nonaggression treaty to be implemented by the dissolution of the North Atlantic Treaty Organization (NATO) and the Warsaw Pact. Leonid Brezhnev proposed a many-faceted plan for the Persian Gulf area that would have greatly reduced tension there. At crucial times, the Soviets have called for banning particular systems, such as neutron bombs, nuclear-armed submarines, and space-based weapons.[30]

We may question the motives of the Soviets in making these proposals; they have doubtless varied from time to time. In evaluating their sincerity, we should bear in mind the incentives mentioned earlier. We may also analyze their past record in arms sessions and solicit the judgment of those who have dealt with them. In specific cases, the best way to find out if they mean business is to take up their offers and try them out.

Concerning the actual negotiations, the testimony of Marshall Shulman is especially significant. He has studied the Soviet Union for nearly forty years, made about thirty trips there, and served as adviser on Soviet affairs to Secretaries of State Acheson, Vance, and Muskie. At present, he is director of the Harriman Institute for Advanced Study of the Soviet Union at Columbia University. In April 1984 he wrote:

> *In the SALT talks, it [the Soviet Union] offered considerably more major concessions than did the United States; it was also prepared to agree that no new land-based intercontinental missiles be allowed, had we been willing. . . . The Russians were stubborn bargainers, but they manifested a serious interest in limiting the nuclear competition.[31]*

Herbert York, adviser to the federal government in several arms control capacities, published in 1983 a historical review of U.S.-Soviet negotiations. After listing several concessions that the Soviets had made in the Strategic Arms Limitations Talks (SALT), he concluded: "The U.S.S.R. has apparently made these concessions and others in a serious spirit of compromise in order to produce a mutually beneficial result."[32] In the winter of 1978–79, the Soviets stayed out of the Vietnam-Chinese border war "because they did not want to scuttle SALT during the final months of the negotiations," according to U.S. experts on Soviet affairs.[33] In 1979 they withdrew some 20,000 troops and 1,000 tanks from the European theater in an effort to reverse the arms race there.[34]

Warnke, Shulman, and York are by no means alone in regarding the Soviets as serious negotiators who genuinely desire arms reduction. Many others have expressed similar judgments, including J. David Singer, director of the correlates of war project at the University of Michigan; Arthur Macy Cox, author of several books on U.S.-Soviet relations; Fred Warner Neal, professor of government at the Claremont Graduate School; William Scranton, former U.N. ambassador; and Brent Scowcroft, foreign policy adviser to President Reagan.[35] Their assessment is aptly summarized by Everett Mendelsohn, professor of the history of science at Harvard University: "Recent conversations in the Soviet Union with high level government advisors indicate that the Soviets are very serious about arms control and reduction."[36]

In discussing the Soviet Union, I have been referring frequently to especially qualified authorities. This is because most people in the United States, including myself, must rely on those who have had relevant experience, and it is important to realize that the views expressed here are not just the opinions of a few individuals. We have been subjected to so much criticism of the Soviet Union, some of it justified, that the more hopeful aspects need to be given the credibility they deserve.

Unfortunately, U.S. policymakers have often summarily rejected Soviet arms control overtures without considering them seriously enough to learn whether they were genuine and practical. I have records of twelve specific instances of this. A typical example occurred on October 6, 1979, when Brezhnev proposed to reduce Warsaw Pact troops, tanks, and SS-20 missiles in Eastern Europe, provided we did not add nuclear weapons in Europe. Instead of exploring the offer, President Carter and National Security Adviser Zbigniew Brzezinski abruptly rejected it.[37] A common excuse given for such rejections is that the proposal is "nothing new." Indeed, this is sometimes the case: we have rejected a similar proposal before. If we really want to reduce the threat of nuclear war, we need to explore every possible route to that goal.

5. Take a realistic view of trusting the Soviets. We must not be deterred by claims that "you can't trust the Russians." It is true that statements of government officials cannot always be accepted at face value. Soviet diplomats have lied to U.S. officials, notably in denying the presence of missile bases in Cuba in 1962. We have lied to them—regarding U-2 flights, for instance. But this does not justify refusing to build a relationship that will lessen the tendency to lie and that will facilitate joint efforts to establish peace. Our task is to forge agreements that, so far as possible, satisfy the interests of both parties and provide incentives for each side to comply.

Those with a special ax to grind charge that the Soviet Union habitually violates treaties, whereas the United States is blameless. Fortunately, U.S. negotiators and the Standing Consultative Commission (SCC) that monitors compliance report equally good records on each side. In 1980 the Defense Department, the State Department, the Joint Chiefs of Staff, and the Arms Control and Disarmament Agency declared that "Soviet compliance performance under 14 arms control agreements signed since 1959 has been good."[38] Among the individuals and agencies that have testified, regarding their particular areas of expertise, to satisfactory Soviet compliance are Thomas Watson, former ambassador to the Soviet Union; SALT negotiator Gerard Smith; Kosta Tsipis of the Program in Science and Technology for International Security at Massachusetts Institute of Technology; Senator Daniel Patrick Moynihan; David Emery, arms control deputy director; Henry Kissinger; Cyrus Vance; the Center for Foreign Policy Development at Brown University; and the Center for Defense Information.[39] There have been borderline cases and possibly some infractions on both sides, but all have been successfully resolved and none has threatened the security of either side.

Beginning in January 1984, the Reagan Administration has several times, in unprecedented fashion, publicly charged the Soviet Union with cheating, claiming that this raised questions about the worth of arms control agreements. Space is lacking here to deal thoroughly with the issue, but certain points should be made. During this same period, the United States has moved ahead with the Strategic Defense Initiative (Star Wars) that threatens to violate the Antiballistic Missile (ABM) Treaty. This will be easier to do if the public can be convinced that the Soviets fail to honor their agreements. In a joint press conference in January 1984, Gerard Smith, Paul Warnke, and Herbert Scoville declared: "Presidential public accusations of bad faith before all consultative or diplomatic avenues have been exhausted only prejudice the eventual resolution of the issues, and make more difficult . . . the

47

achievement of our basic security objective of reducing the risk of nuclear war."[40]

In late 1984, the President released to the public a summary of a General Advisory Committee (GAC) report to the Arms Control and Disarmament Agency. The report accuses the Soviets of several arms control violations and implies that negotiation with the Soviets does more harm than good. It should be noted that GAC members are appointed by the President, all twelve of them opposed SALT II, and seven are current or former members of the Committee on the Present Danger. Thomas Longstreth, senior analyst at the Arms Control Association, has written a detailed indictment of the GAC (as now constituted) and its findings. Among other things, he observes that the "five previous administrations, both Republican and Democratic, reviewed the same activities and body of evidence but reached conclusions different from those of the current GAC."[41]

It is not surprising that the Soviets have reacted to the President's charges by producing lists of alleged U.S. violations. In an atmosphere of mutual recrimination, it is difficult to resolve issues of genuine concern, such as the possibility that the radar facility being built by the Soviets in Siberia or some being constructed by the United States may violate the ABM treaty. In the future, as in the past, we need to handle these matters unobtrusively through such channels as the SCC.

Despite their limitations, arms control agreements have the potential to enhance national security by restricting weapons development on both sides. Our task is to improve the process rather than tear it down. To do this we need to keep refining our verification techniques and raising the level of mutual confidence. Those who have been involved with the Soviets assure us that it can be done.

Chapter III.

FOREIGN POLICY AND ARMS CONTROL— A NEW APPROACH

THE PURPOSE OF the first chapter is to show that seeking to deter a potential enemy by piling up nuclear weapons moves us closer to the war we are trying to avoid. The aim of the second chapter is to provide a realistic assessment of the Soviet threat and suggest ways to achieve a constructive relationship with the Soviet Union in order to reduce the risk of nuclear war. The conclusions reached in both chapters point to the need for a critical appraisal of current U.S. foreign policy, followed by suggestions for a practical approach that will provide hope for a more secure world through genuine arms reduction.

Many analysts agree that U.S. foreign policy has not achieved its primary goal: greater national security. It has failed to achieve the reductions in nuclear weapons that would constitute a step toward that goal. Why is this the case? How is our policy inadequate and how may it be improved? Our perspective has been too limited: U.S. foreign policy has failed to deal realistically with the radically new situation created by nuclear weapons. Painfully aware of this, military historian Michael Howard recently declared that he had quit reading the calculations of nuclear strategists because they were so engaged in theory spinning as to be divorced from reality.[1] After examining four respects in which this is evident, I shall advocate a different approach to foreign policy,

49

with special reference to arms control. Although my focus is on the United States, most of what follows applies also to the Soviet Union and other major powers.

INADEQUATE CONSIDERATION OF OUR PERIL

My first criticism is that policymakers fail to give adequate consideration to our peril. Although occasionally according it lip service, they make decisions that amount to denying its reality. The degree of our danger becomes evident when we raise two questions: How destructive would a nuclear war be? How likely is it to occur? The catastrophic effects of a nuclear war are so well known that I shall not detail them here. But how likely is it to erupt?

As stated in chapter I, unless the United States drastically changes its policy, it is only a matter of time before the holocaust engulfs us all. Practically every well-informed individual with no special ax to grind agrees that our situation is extremely precarious. We have been warned of this by international affairs scholars at Harvard, Princeton, and Columbia, and by a vast array of scientists, former ambassadors to the Soviet Union, and retired military officers, who are no longer constrained by official positions.[2] Yet as one studies the plans of Pentagon and Defense Department officials, one feels a strange sense of unreality. They seem to be living in a fantasy world where nuclear war can be fought successfully to defend national interests. And they keep trying to assure us that our military might will keep war from occurring. President Reagan even claimed in 1984 that we were in less danger than we were four years earlier.[3]

Consider this: In response to the U.S. deployment of Pershing II and cruise missiles in Western Europe, the Soviets have stationed new, advanced missiles in East Germany and Czechoslovakia. They have also brought larger, more modern nuclear-armed submarines (Delta-2) closer to U.S.

shores.[4] Anatoly Alexandrov, president of the Soviet Academy of Sciences, has warned that the Soviets plan to establish a launch-under-attack system to ensure that nuclear missiles will be fired automatically in response to what *Novosti,* an official Soviet news agency, refers to as "practically any provocation or even accident."[5]

Alan Romberg, of the State Department, minimized the significance of the Soviet deployment, complacently asserting that missiles have long been aimed at Western Europe and the United States.[6] When Soviet Defense Minister Dimitri Ustinov announced that sea-based missiles could now reach U.S. cities in ten minutes, Caspar Weinberger scoffed: "I was amused at Marshall Ustinov's statement because he's referring to conditions that have existed . . . for about 15, 18 years."[7] It will be less amusing when the missiles, many times more powerful than the Hiroshima bomb, obliterate 100 million Americans.

The failure of U.S. decision-makers to face up to our peril naturally affects our foreign policy. A realistic appraisal of our situation is essential for sound judgment. When the official doctrine is that nuclear war is survivable or unlikely to happen, we will take risks that would otherwise be rejected. Protecting U.S. access to Persian Gulf oil, for example, would not be worth the risk of extinguishing the human species.

INADEQUATE CONSIDERATION OF EFFECTS OF U.S. ACTIONS

My second criticism of U.S. foreign policy is that it fails to take a realistic account of the effects of U.S. actions—notably the probable Soviet responses. In chapter I, I noted that our deployment of MIRVed (multiple independently targeted re-entry vehicle) missiles spurred the Soviets to do likewise, decreasing our security. Further examples of short-sightedness abound. Our bellicose blusterings strengthen Soviet hard-liners and weaken the moderate elements in their political hierarchy.[8] This impedes constructive diplomatic efforts. U.S. plans to destroy Soviet command and communication centers at the outset of hostilities provide another case in point. Only if such centers remain intact would there be a chance to prevent chaos and bring the war to an early close.

Equally serious are the alliances and agreements that the United States has made, such as the commitment to NATO nations—to consider an attack on any of them as an attack on the United States—and assurances we have given to Israel and South Korea. In the nuclear age, entering on such agreements makes our own citizens hostages—dependent on the restraint of foreign officials. It is not enough to cite certain advantages of these commitments. Short-term benefits must be weighed against long-term perils. Seldom has this characterized U.S. foreign policy. As George Ball, former undersecretary of state, has lamented, we pursue our policy "with inadequate thought and little foresight."[9]

FAILURE TO TAKE INNOVATIVE APPROACH TO NEGOTIATIONS

A third basic weakness in U.S. foreign policy has been the failure to take the sort of bold, new approach to arms control that the existence of nuclear weapons requires. The need for a fresh point of view is expressed succinctly by Sidney Drell: "The record of past arms control negotiations . . . has seen the number of strategic nuclear warheads triple after thirteen years of negotiation."[10]

The reasons for this dismal record are not to be found in some ineptness in pursuing the numbers game. The experts have served us well in comparing launchers, throw weight, and warheads. Our failure lies in our attitudes, perceptions, and (sometimes covert) goals. Hence the discussion of arms control in this chapter is set in the context of a critique of U.S. foreign policy as a whole. When we recognize our peril, our short-sightedness, and our failure to consider fresh approaches to national security, we are in a position to acknowledge several reasons for the lack of significant arms reductions.

1. The arms race mentality. We keep fearing that we are, or will be, behind. We imagine a bomber gap, a missile gap, or a window of vulnerability. Under such conditions, we are unwilling to bargain seriously, rationalizing that we should only negotiate from strength. Yet our strategy precludes bargaining when we are ahead, lest we jeopardize our lead. And because the weapons are different on both sides, we can never be sure that the two sides are equal.

2. The technological momentum. We are not willing to be restricted in pursuing new types of weapons development. This is partly because of the inherent momentum in arms research and partly through fear of being surprised by a technological breakthrough of a rival nation. Thus the U.S. 1984–88 Defense Guidance document specifies that the United States "must ensure that treaties and agreements do not foreclose opportunities to develop these [military space] capabilities."[11] In other words, arms control will be tolerated so long as it does not control arms.

3. The sharp deal mentality. Our attitude is generally that of seeking to gain an advantage over our rival rather than to reduce weapons. Comparing arms negotiations with driving a sharp business deal, Secretary of State George Shultz has warned that the United States should not appear too eager: "We must be very careful that we don't somehow get ourselves in a position of feeling that it is very important to get an agreement. The minute you see another guy really wants an agreement you've got him."[12] Richard Perle, assistant secretary of defense for international security policy, favored President Reagan's zero option because it would "put the Soviets on the defensive."[13] We assume that our safety is enhanced as the other nation's is decreased. In the nuclear age, however, the only real security is shared security.

4. *The bargaining chip rationalization.* We deploy new types of weaponry on the ground that they will be bargaining chips. This pretext has been effectively demolished by arms control expert Jane Sharp, of Cornell University, who writes that alleged bargaining chips do not

> —*Cause recalcitrant adversaries to negotiate.*
> —*Soften the adversary's negotiating position.*
> —*End up being cashed in . . . for weapons systems on the other side.*
> —*Or facilitate the conclusion of arms control agreements not negotiable otherwise.*
>
> *Evidence from arms control experiences with the Soviet Union overwhelmingly suggests that U.S. weapons systems acquired to beef up bargaining strength will:*
> —*Delay . . . bargaining by the other side.*
> —*Toughen the adversary's negotiating stance.*
> —*Remain as part of the permanent arsenal.*
> —*Ensure that an agreement will be at higher force levels than would otherwise have been possible.*[14]

5. *The effect of new weapons systems.* We develop and deploy new weapons without sufficient regard for their negative impact on arms control. The arms control impact statements submitted annually to Congress by the Administration did not prevent the U.S. deployment of cruise missiles in Europe. Yet these missiles are only about twenty feet long and can easily be concealed in trucks or haystacks. Moreover, they are mobile, are inexpensive enough to be produced in quantity, and can be launched in either nuclear or conventional versions. It is practically impossible to verify their existence, much less their numbers. Because U.S. policymakers refuse to negotiate any treaty that cannot be verified with virtually 100 percent certainty, deploying this missile strikes a serious blow at arms control.[15]

6. *The no-risk or compromise mentality.* Insistence on well-nigh perfect verification exemplifies a major reason the United States has not halted the arms race: We have been unwilling to make even minor sacrifices for peace. For example, in negotiations with the Soviet Union, the United States has refused to take British and French nuclear weapons into account. This has been justified by Robert Dean, deputy director of the Bureau of Politico-Military Affairs in the State Department, on the ground that if they were counted and either of those countries then increased the number of their missiles, we would have to decrease ours.[16] Is this a sufficient reason to impede negotiations that could reduce the risk of nuclear war?

Many examples attest U.S. reluctance to compromise or undergo any sacrifice in order to achieve weapons reduction— despite widespread recognition that if the arms race continues, a nuclear holocaust is nearly inevitable. The effect this attitude had on the comprehensive test ban talks has been pointed out by Gerard Smith, chief U.S. delegate to SALT I, currently chairman of the Arms Control Association:

> *More than 20 years ago Nikita Khrushchev wrote President Kennedy that since the verification issue was bogging down the talks, the Soviets would accept three on-site inspections a year. We then asked for seven. What a difference there would now be in the military confrontation if all nuclear tests had ended during the Kennedy Administration when the United States was far ahead. There would now be no MIRVs, no MX and perhaps no cruise missiles, no Pershings—and all for want of four annual inspections.[17]*

No wonder Harold Macmillan, British Prime Minister, exclaimed to President Eisenhower regarding the comprehensive test ban: "We ought to take risks for so great a prize!"[18]

It comes down to the fact that U.S. policymakers have lacked the will, the resolve, to reduce U.S. arsenals. Thus Averell Harriman, former ambassador to the Soviet Union, refers to the *serious doubts in the minds of many about whether there ever was an intention to reach any reasonable agreement. Negotiations have been treated as a forum for propaganda, an occasion for invective, a mask to cover new deployments and an arena to gain advantage—rather than as a path to human survival on this planet.*[19]

This is borne out by official statements of the place of arms control in U.S. foreign policy. According to Caspar Weinberger, the purpose of arms control is "to complement and enhance national security."[20] Despite occasional lip service to the contrary, Weinberger and other government spokespersons do not intend to achieve this by reducing U.S. arsenals. They conceive of national security strictly in terms of military superiority. Arms control is considered an integral part of our defense program, which depends on military might.[21] When he was director of the Arms Control and Disarmament Agency, Eugene Rostow made this quite clear. He referred to the MX, Pershing II, cruise missiles, Trident II, anti-satellite systems, and chemical weapons as programs that "will permit us to pursue arms control objectives in a way that will enhance our security."[22] It is clear that genuine arms reduction and the arms control envisaged by our leaders are contradictory.

INADEQUATE CONSIDERATION
OF ALTERNATIVE PROPOSALS

My final criticism of our current policy, which accounts in part for the criticisms leveled earlier, is that U.S. decision-makers fail to consider adequately the ideas of well-informed individuals outside their immediate circle. This becomes evident as we note the relationship to foreign policy of three categories of individuals. The first group consists of those who have the power to make the decisions: the President, the Secretary of State, the Secretary of Defense, the arms control negotiators, the Joint Chiefs of Staff, and their colleagues.

Most of those in the second category are former policymakers. These are at least as knowledgeable as the first group but are generally not currently in positions of power. They include, for example, retired military personnel, former ambassadors, and former cabinet members. Some are associated with think tanks like the Center for Defense Information, the World Policy Institute, or the Institute for Policy Studies. Among them are Paul Warnke, Gerard Smith, Sidney Drell, Jerome Wiesner, George Kennan, McGeorge Bundy, Thomas Watson, and Cyrus Vance. They are well represented in such journals as *Foreign Affairs, International Security,* and *Foreign Policy.* The extent to which their views are considered seriously varies. But when they differ significantly from Administration policy, they receive scant attention.

Those in the third category may be designated "independent critics." They may never have been part of the official bureaucracy, but they have become well versed on the issues. They are usually associated with organizations like Physicians for Social Responsibility, The Committee for a Sane Nuclear Policy, American Friends Service Committee, and Fellowship of Reconciliation. They are almost totally ignored by the policymakers. This has been noted by Thomas Powers. Concerning those who have warned that nuclear war is practically inevitable if we continue our present course, he observes: "Not one of them shows any sign whatever of being taken to heart by the only men who count—the budget-makers and diplomats who buy the arms and issue the white papers."[23]

Those in the second and third categories have produced many statements, articles, and books reflecting wide experience, hard common sense, and penetrating insight. Yet U.S. policymakers seem scarcely aware of the suggestions or implications for policy found in this literature. The few remarks that the President and the Secretary of Defense make concerning their critics are generally superficial, revealing a woeful lack of understanding.[24]

How many of those who formulate U.S. policy have studied the GRIT literature referred to later in this chapter? How many have read *Common Security,* a report of the Independent Commission on Disarmament and Security Issues, composed of world leaders chaired by the late Olof Palme of Sweden?[25] How many have considered seriously the proposals advanced by Randall Forsberg, of the Institute for Defense and Disarmament Studies? How many have studied with care the Report of the Alternative Defence Commission—*Defence Without the Bomb?*[26]

Have our leaders given real thought to the ideas and proposals of George Kennan, one of the most informed persons in the United States concerning our relations with the Soviet Union? In view of the failure of the war system in the past and our precarious position in the present, how much attention has been given to alternative, nonviolent methods of defense as explored in the writings of Gene Sharp?[27]

REQUIREMENTS FOR A CONSTRUCTIVE APPROACH

If we are ever to achieve the sort of arms control that will reduce arms and decrease the likelihood of nuclear war, a new approach is needed. Even former National Security Adviser Zbigniew Brzezinski has admitted that "a very strong argument can be made that we have come to the end of the road in traditional arms control approaches."[28] I turn now to a more hopeful policy and then consider a strategy that is being advocated with increasing frequency by competent analysts who are not part of the present bureaucracy.

At the outset, we must recognize our peril—that if we fail, we are doomed. The first requirement, then, is to be willing to make some sacrifices for the sake of survival. We may need to pay a price for peace. It follows that we should be willing to enter into constructive agreements even if compliance cannot be verified 100 percent. Certainly any risk we take will be less than that of our present policy, whereby we jeopardize our very existence.

The second requirement is to make proposals that the rival nation will recognize as being fair—naive as this may seem! Such a radical approach would doubtless arouse suspicions on the other side, but these could be overcome in time. If necessary, we should be willing to take a slight loss in the numbers game. To be able to destroy the Soviets a few less times than they could destroy us would not affect our security, even in the military sense. Instead of haggling over details, we should strive for a significant breakthrough in negotiations. This requires that we keep our main goal firmly in mind: to stop the arms race and reduce weapons, rather than to gain an advantage over our rival.

A PRACTICAL PROCESS OF ARMS REDUCTION

If we can bring U.S. policymakers to adopt this more creative approach, we shall be in a position to participate in a process that is being advocated with increasing frequency. It consists of taking "independent initiatives." This would not be a substitute for bilateral or multilateral negotiations, but would help the negotiations move forward. It has been described by Robert Johansen, Senior Fellow, World Policy Institute, in his pamphlet *Toward a Dependable Peace;* by Paul Walker, former arms control director of the Union of Concerned Scientists, in *Seizing the Initiative: First Steps to Disarmament;* and by Charles E. Osgood, professor at the University of Illinois.[29] Osgood calls it Graduated and Reciprocated Initiatives in Tension Reduction (GRIT).

This approach consists of a carefully planned freeze or reduction of some aspect of a nation's military program or weapons system and an invitation to the rival nation to respond in like fashion. If the rival nation fails to do so, the interrupted process can be resumed. If the rival responds favorably, a further step can be taken. For this process to gain acceptance and be undertaken, certain essential features must be recognized and certain procedures followed. These are spelled out by Osgood in the *Bulletin of the Atomic Scientists,* which informs much of the following.[30]

The first initiatives should not jeopardize a nation's military defense capability. This poses no problem, since we have such tremendous overkill capacity. Members of the Boston Study Group of distinguished arms analysts contend quite convincingly that the United States could cut its defense budget by $50 billion annually without loss of military effectiveness.[31] It is important also that the initiatives not be too far-reaching and that they be graduated in risk according to the reciprocation expected.

Although the program must be conceived and implemented with care, it should be stressed both at home and abroad that it represents a basic change of direction. Our total foreign policy should harmonize with the change. Initiatives aimed at reducing tension and inducing reciprocal responses should not be negated by threats or arms escalation at other points. To enable the public and officials in both nations to perceive the initiatives as part of a larger pattern, they should be announced well in advance of their execution.

When the program is announced and when the first steps are taken, the rival nation should be invited to reciprocate in a manner of its own choosing. The invitation must be issued carefully to avoid the impression that a threat is being made. In view of past attitudes and actions, we must expect such a change of policy to be met with skepticism. There is every reason to expect this gradually to be allayed, however, for it would be very much to the advantage of the Soviet Union and other nations to reciprocate, once major reductions have attested our sincerity. Public opinion throughout the world would provide powerful support to such action.

Each step in the process should be as unambiguous as possible and subject to verification. It should be continued long enough to give the rival nation time to respond favorably. If it becomes clear that a particular step will not be reciprocated, we could abandon it. But if little sacrifice would be involved, it would generally be wiser to continue in the new direction in order to create a better atmosphere.

Psychologist Fred H. Wright has analyzed the research in his field relevant to this issue. It indicates clearly that a change of behavior by one party tends to produce a change of attitude by both parties, which facilitates modification of behavior by both. Applying this to the issue of arms reduction, psychologists Charles E. Osgood and Jerome Frank and sociologist Amitai Etzioni cite several historical examples to show that independent initiatives produce more favorable results than do multilateral negotiations.[32]

Undertaking independent initiatives is not new. An account of several past instances is provided by Franklin A. Long in the *Bulletin of the Atomic Scientists*.[33] These have usually been isolated cases, not part of an integrated plan carried out according to the guidelines specified earlier. On the whole, responses by other nations have been encouraging. Probably the most notable series of such initiatives and responses occurred between 1958 and 1963, culminating in the Limited Test Ban Treaty.[34]

In the last decade or so, several discerning individuals and groups have advocated independent initiatives of various types. They include The World Without War Council; the Center for Defense Information; Lloyd Dumas, professor at the University of Texas-Dallas; Jerome Wiesner; Victor Weisskopf, of the Massachusetts Institute of Technology; and Thomas C. Schelling.[35] These proposals have been ignored, rather than answered, by advocates of military escalation. To be truly responsible, we must give serious consideration to them. It is very likely that only decisive initiatives will provide the breakthrough needed to replace suspicion and rigidity with trust and flexibility. Robert Johansen has expressed the view of a growing number: "Because U.S. officials in effect pursue national military advantages rather than mutual security gains, they fail to grasp the most powerful and versatile bargaining lever available to negotiators to achieve arms reductions: the independent initiative."[36]

AGENDA FOR A SAFER WORLD

In determining the specific initiatives to take, the basic premise should be that our own security will be enhanced by the creation of common security—a world in which both superpowers, and therefore all people, are more secure. Fortunately, many practical and thought-provoking proposals have been presented for the achievement of a more peaceful world. In addition to *Common Security, Defence Without the Bomb*, and the other sources mentioned earlier, are such agencies as the Friends Committee on National Legislation, the Council for a Livable World, and the Union of Concerned Scientists, which keep producing and updating appropriate agendas.

Many such proposals, typically dealt with in arms control negotiations, would lend themselves to independent initiatives. Such steps as the following would greatly enhance security: a moratorium on the testing and deployment of nuclear weapons, with a comprehensive test ban treaty (CTBT) as the goal; a moratorium on the militarization of outer space; a moratorium on the flight testing of strategic nuclear delivery vehicles; a moratorium on the production of weapons-grade fissile materials; a significant percentage reduction of the military budget.

Since the Soviets unilaterally ceased testing for a considerable period starting on August 6, 1985, and invited the United States to do the same, they would surely join us in the first of these steps. Their opposition to the U.S. Strategic Defense Initiative (Star Wars) program means that they would join us in the second. The U.S. Administration, as I write, is unwilling to adopt these measures. This situation could change, however. In 1985, growing public pressure throughout the world impelled 121 member states of the U.N. General Assembly to approve a comprehensive test ban. Considerable pressure is mounting on U.S. policymakers to resume negotiations to that end.

In addition to independent initiatives aimed at reversing

the arms race, joint actions should be taken with the Soviet Union and with other nations to alleviate international tensions. These would include forging agreements regarding relationships with Third World nations, creating an international crisis-stability center, and engaging in a variety of confidence-building activities.

While my purpose has been to deal primarily with attitudes and points of view, rather than with detailed proposals, I have indicated steps that could be taken in the near future. The question naturally arises, "How can such changes be effected?" It is one thing to suggest a course of action—quite a different matter to get it implemented. I shall not repeat the constructive methods advocated by such organizations as the American Friends Service Committee, the War Resisters League, and the Fellowship of Reconciliation. Yet I do suggest two ways the momentum to war could be reversed: through enlightened leadership and through the power of the people.

Look first at the importance of leadership. Just before Franklin D. Roosevelt was elected, if someone had predicted the social reforms and welfare measures that were later achieved during his Administration, the predictions would have been dismissed as beyond the realm of possibility. But they became reality. As described in Alan Wolfe's book *The Rise and Fall of the Soviet Threat*, the peak periods of anti-Soviet hostility have come when Democratic Presidents felt the need to appease right-wing pressure groups.[37] Initiatives in the direction of peace have been made by conservative Republicans, like Eisenhower and Nixon, who were not subject to such pressures. Actually, either a Republican or a Democratic President could impel us on the road to peace, especially if he or she were to perceive that this would guarantee a niche in history as a great leader.

In any case, the direction we take will depend on the power of the people, for governments rest ultimately on popular support. Daniel Webster proclaimed: "Nothing will ruin the country if the people undertake its safety." This is good news. We have it in our power to achieve peace. The power of the people produced civil rights legislation, the Atmospheric Test Ban treaty, the ABM treaty, the cancellation by Nixon of plans to atom-bomb Hanoi, and the end of the Vietnam war. Public opinion caused Prime Minister Margaret Thatcher to reject a U.S. offer to deploy deep-strike conventional weapons in Britain. In an article discussing five crucial decisions that the United States made in nuclear weapons policy since World War II, Sidney Drell concludes:

> *The importance of an informed and effective arms-control constituency cannot be overestimated. . . . In three cases there was no public involvement (and no effective political pressure), and we lost serious opportunities to halt or reduce the growing dangers of nuclear weapons. In two cases there was public participation, and important and enduring arms restraints were negotiated with the Soviet Union.*[38]

It seems to me that a majority of the American people is becoming aware of the folly of our present course and will support the sort of positive steps I have suggested. Many able people who may not be committed to nonviolence recognize that our present military escalation goes far beyond what they consider legitimate armed defense. A sizable number are retired military or government officials who can now speak freely. A coalition appears to be developing that will influence policymakers greatly to reduce weaponry and take other steps that will make the world vastly much safer. The farther we go in this new direction, the more insight we shall gain for additional progress and the more secure we shall become. All peace-loving people can unite in this effort; it must be our near-term agenda in order to survive.

For the long pull, however, we must go farther. Although opposed to the present arms race, most Americans still think of military defense as our ultimate security. Foreign policy analysts who favor genuine arms reduction would still rely on "minimum armed deterrence." This is because neither the general public nor the analysts see a viable alternative. As long as this is the case, war will be a possibility. And because we shall always retain the knowledge of modern weaponry— nuclear, high-powered conventional, chemical, and bacteriological—war could escalate to the dimensions of a holocaust. This makes our age unlike any that preceded it. It is doubtful, therefore, that the process I have advocated up to this point would be far-reaching enough to provide long-term security. We would still be living on borrowed time. With good luck, however, it would give us leeway to develop a public constituency to support the measures needed for lasting peace.

The orientation for these further steps is provided in this remarkable statement by George Kennan:

> *I am now bound to say that while the earliest possible elimination of nuclear weaponry is of . . . vital importance in my eyes . . . , this would not be enough, in itself, to give Western Civilization even an adequate chance of survival. War itself, as a means of settling differences . . . will have to be . . . ruled out; and with it there will have to be dismantled (for without this the whole outlawing of war would be futile) the greater part of the vast military establishments.*[39]

This is an awesome task—but no more so than the Manhattan Project that developed the atom bomb or the Strategic Defense Initiative (Star Wars) effort. It requires two developments.

The first is to establish the necessary conditions for peace. Just as the international scene in a world at war becomes adapted to the war, so now we must create a climate conducive to peace—both internationally and within nations. This would affect the conduct of the economy, education, scientific research, the corporate world, international trade— in fact, practically every aspect of the common life. It would include developing effective, peaceful means to adjudicate international disputes, as advocated by the World Federalist Association and its offshoot, the Commission on Respect for

International Law. The Exploratory Project on the Conditions of Peace (Expro) is engaged in a pioneering, creative effort to envisage a peaceful world and the specific steps needed to attain it.

None of us working on such projects anticipates a utopia. Even in the best of worlds, problems will remain and conflicts will occur that are not satisfactorily arbitrated. A combination of the measures I have advocated constitutes, in a sense, a substitute for war. But the felt need for defense and for war as a last resort is so deeply ingrained in us that people will insist on a more direct and specific type of defense. A second needed development, then, in tandem with establishing the conditions for peace, is to prepare ultimately for a nonmilitary, nonviolent method of defense. That there may be such a method will come as a surprise to many. Sometimes called social, or civilian-based, defense, it will be examined in chapter V. In the modern world, it may well be the only practical way to defend a major power.

It often appears that moral considerations are largely irrelevant in matters of war and peace, but deep within all of us is the need to justify our actions by ethical standards. We shall be more likely to adopt the radical measures advocated in this chapter and in chapter V if we see them as morally imperative. Such an alternative approach commends itself because modern war (and by implication U.S. foreign policy) is not only impractical, but deeply immoral.

Chapter IV.

CAN MODERN WAR BE MORAL?

UP TO THIS point, I have dealt with major issues of war and peace from a common sense, practical perspective. Now I want to focus on the most important question, although it is seldom recognized as such. The leading foreign affairs journals contain countless articles dealing with endless details regarding warheads, throw weight, launchers, MIRVs, GLCMs, SLCMs, and a host of other acronyms. The articles are informative, but they do not satisfy Sidney Drell. He laments:

> *It is not enough just to discuss and analyze the nuts and bolts of weapons technology. . . . The question of whether the use of nuclear weapons can be justified on any ethical grounds is rarely heard. . . . These are weapons of mass destruction, and the possibility of ever using such weapons raises fundamental ethical issues that should be faced at the center of our national . . . discussion.[1]*

How often are they faced? How often have we questioned the morality of planning to kill millions of our fellow humans— either in a first strike or in retaliation for the adversary's strike?

I have recently heard talks by a colonel in the army and by a Defense Department official, each of whom prefaced his remarks with the admission: "Of course I am not dealing with moral issues." The antisubmarine warfare operator of Navy Air Squadron 24 has a crucial function in the U.S. capability of striking first with nuclear weapons that would slaughter nearly every man, woman, and child in the Soviet Union. He says about his role: "I get fairly well paid, I have a beautiful home, and I'd be hard-pressed to do as well on the outside and still have an interesting job. I just love it."[2]

These reactions are so typical they compel us to ask; "Why raise the question of right and wrong?" One answer is that in so doing, we shall focus on the major problem of our time from a new perspective, which could cast fresh light on it. Another reason is that our capacity for moral discrimination is what makes us human. It distinguishes us from animals and machines. Nuclear power makes no moral distinction between providing homes with electricity and destroying 100,000 persons in Hiroshima. If we were to ignore the moral issue, we might well ask, as one writer has expressed it, "Are we no better than our most technically sophisticated implements of death?"[3]

In referring to "we" and "our," I mean all of us. It is virtually impossible to live in a highly militarized nation like the United States without sharing the collective responsibility. It is often claimed that if the common people had their way, wars would not occur, or would be conducted in more humane fashion. This is a matter of speculation, but events of the past 150 years and some recent polls cause me to question that assumption. The belligerence of the policymakers often reflects the pressures of the people, and military operations are, to a great extent, determined by civilian officials. In discussing the strategic bombing policy of World War II, Michael Walzer, of the Institute for Advanced Study at Princeton, concludes: "Explicit moral disagreement developed most importantly among the professional soldiers involved in the decision-making process."[4]

We are all in this boat together; neither the common people, nor the policymakers, nor the military can point an accusing finger at the others. But perhaps we should all point at ourselves, for I want now to indicate several ways that our actions in World War II and our plans for World War III constitute gross violations of ethical principles. Then I shall explore some explanations for our present policy, with special reference to the defense of freedom. Finally, I shall contend that the moral imperative requires that we join George Kennan and Robert J. Lifton in calling for the eventual abandonment of war as a method of national defense, trusting that there must be a better way.[5]

HOW WE ARE BREAKING
THE MORAL LAW

1. Violating the sanctity of human life. The first way that we are breaking the moral law should be obvious, but it needs emphasizing. We are callously disregarding the sanctity of personality and the intrinsic value of human life. When the Nazis dropped their bombs on Britain in World War II, the Western world was aghast at such barbarity. But then the Allies, as a deliberate policy, massacred civilians—hundreds of thousands—in Hamburg, Dresden, Tokyo, Hiroshima, Nagasaki. In defeating Hitler, we practiced Hitler's ethics. Now we are ready to kill untold millions in World War III.

"Thou shalt not kill." Does not a voice in all of us warn that we must not disobey that commandment? If the killing of a single individual is a tragedy, what about the declaration of a navy captain that people were getting too concerned about nuclear war for, after all, "only 500 million people would be killed"?[6] The impending war is frequently referred to as mass suicide. This is not literally correct; we shall be killing not ourselves, but each other. It is more accurately designated mass murder.

Let us think further about what killing people means. Goodness, truth, beauty, and love—these are the basic values. But they have meaning only for human beings. One of the most significant ethical insights is that each person, as a

69

bearer of values, is an end in himself or herself—not just a means to an end. When human life is taken lightly, people are reduced to a subhuman level. Enemy soldiers are considered "huns" or "gooks"—scarcely people like ourselves. Our own armed forces are brutalized and treated as instruments.

The war system requires that all of us suppress our human, moral feelings in order to maintain the resolve to annihilate the enemy. In 1949, scientists Enrico Fermi and Isador Rabi submitted a statement to the Atomic Energy Commission regarding whether to develop the H-bomb. They wrote: "It is clear that the use of such a weapon cannot be justified on any ethical ground which gives a human being a certain individuality and dignity. . . . It is necessarily an evil thing considered in any light."[7]

Before being appointed to his present position in the Department of Defense, Fred Iklé declared that the sensitivity of our strategic planners "to the distinction between combatants and civilians—long cultivated through civilizing centuries—had become dulled by the strategic bombing in World War II" and caused them to view the mass killing of noncombatants as a "bonus effect" that nuclear bombing would have in World War III. Referring to our "moral perversity," Iklé added that our policy rested on "a form of warfare universally condemned since the Dark Ages—the mass killing of hostages."[8]

Even before we engage in it, our acquiescence in preparation for such slaughter has an effect of which we are scarcely aware. It subtly dulls our capacity for moral discrimination and contributes to what the philosopher Paul Tillich called the plight of our generation—an experience "of disintegration, of a world-wide loss of values and meanings."[9] In his volume *Weapons and Hope*, Freeman Dyson, of the Institute for Advanced Study at Princeton, confirms Tillich's observation:

> *It is immoral for us to base our policy upon the threat to carry out a massacre of innocent people greater than all the massacres in mankind's bloody history. . . . The immorality*

70

*of our policy is a major contributory cause of the feelings of
malaise and alienation which are widespread among
intelligent Americans, and of the feelings of distrust with
which the United States is regarded by people overseas. . . .
An immoral concept not only is bad in itself but also has a
corrosive effect upon our spirits. It deprives us of our self-
respect and of the good opinion of mankind—two things
more important to our survival than invulnerable missiles.[10]*

At the very heart of our society we reject the sacredness
of human personality and sanction killing on a colossal scale.
Is it any wonder that violence increases in our cities, schools,
and homes and that frustrated groups around the world resort
to terrorism?

2. *Violating our stewardship.* A second respect in which
we are breaking the moral law is closely related to the first. A
widely accepted principle is that we are all stewards: of our
lives—what we do; of our talents—how we use them; of our
material possessions; and of the world of nature.

One of the most insidious evils throughout the world is
that when we induct people into the armed forces, we commit
them to kill. In some respects, the military has high ethical
standards, reflected in the West Point motto: *Duty, Honor,
Country.* But in battle, soldiers must commit acts that would
be considered criminal in civilian life. Certain aspects of their
training prepare them for this. The emphasis on authority, on
obeying orders, on conformity, are necessary for the conduct
of war, but they militate against raising questions of right and
wrong. We think of Nazi Germany as being evil because of
Hitler. But what harm could he have done if millions of
German soldiers had not put themselves at his disposal? Think
of the Cuban soldiers who fight anywhere in the world at
Castro's bidding. Think of the U.S. armed forces, willing to
kill Central Americans because the commander in chief wants
to end America's "self-doubt." More ominous are the people
in charge of nuclear weapons, ready to slaughter millions of
civilians. In practice sessions they have already gone through

the preliminary steps, stopping short of turning the final key only when told that these were merely tests. What kind of stewardship of our own persons is that?

In terms of our material resources, think how we could tackle the worldwide problems of poverty, hunger, ignorance, and disease with only a fraction of the wealth devoted to the war machine. As regards the natural environment, instead of enhancing it in the service of human welfare, we are polluting the creation with which we are entrusted. Nuclear explosions have already done immeasurable harm to humans and to our world. The effects of the radiation we are prepared to unleash would be colossal. We recoil in horror at the lack of ethical sensitivity revealed by attempts to minimize this evil by glossing over or misrepresenting the facts. Especially ghastly is the humor of a defense corporation representative who referred with detachment and irony to millions of deaths in nuclear war and added, concerning its genetic effects, that parents may "learn to love two-headed children twice as much."[11]

To the pollution of our world by radiation must be added the effects of chemical and biological warfare. The real nature of this was expressed as early as 1959 by the Department of Health, Education, and Welfare: "Biological warfare is the intentional use of living organisms or their toxic products, to cause death, disability, or damage in man, animals, or plants. The target is man, either by causing his sickness or death or through limitation of his food. . . . BW has been aptly described as public health in reverse."[12] Can this be reconciled with our stewardship of natural resources?

3. Destroying human civilization. A third indictment of our military momentum is that whether we intend it or not, we are preparing to destroy our heritage and the rights of future generations. From a religious perspective, we are presuming to cast off the role of creatures and usurp the prerogatives of God. When we consider the spiritual potential of our fellow human beings, with the capacity for goodness and love; as we contemplate the quest for truth exemplified by the libraries of the world, and the creations of beauty preserved in

72

museums; and as we realize that we are forging the means to destroy it all, can we help but feel a great sadness?

In recent years, several scientists have concluded that we may indeed destroy it all. We cannot predict every detail regarding the effects of nuclear war. Those who have studied the possibility of a nuclear winter, however, agree that the effects of nuclear explosions over cities and forests would be far more catastrophic than previously realized and could cause climatic disturbances that would devastate the world.[13] People like Paul Warnke and scientist Lewis Thomas have been "astonished," "appalled," and "dismayed" that government officials have either ignored or attempted to discredit the studies. An internal memo from the Navy Department did express concern—about what? That the findings may pose "short-term public relations problems."[14]

Do we have the right to risk extinguishing the human species? Is not this exchanging the worship of God for the worship of the H-Bomb—the ultimate blasphemy? Echoing a statement of the American Academy of Religion that our policy is "contrary to the faith and fundamental moral values of the religious traditions of humankind," John Bennett, former president of Union Theological Seminary, recently wrote: "No conceivable issue at stake could justify the risking of human existence or the continuities of civilized life on which the values depend for which people might think they were fighting."[15]

4. Inverting moral distinctions. We contravene the moral law also by engaging in the practice denounced by the prophet Isaiah (5:20):

> *Woe to those who call evil good and good evil,*
> *who put darkness for light and light for darkness.*

On the one hand, we brag that we are standing tall because we are building more instruments of death and can bully smaller nations. On the other hand, peacemakers are often considered subversives. Note the treatment accorded Marjorie Swann, a

New England housewife. When she trespassed on government property while protesting the Omaha missile base, the judge performed his legal right by sentencing her to jail. Then, referring to her absence from home and children during the protest and jail term, he added insult to injury and asserted: "You are a bad mother."

A visitor called at the Swann home shortly before her return. Perhaps a little more dust lay on the parlor floor, although he failed to notice it. Possibly the children had lost a few pounds from the substitute cooking, although it was not evident. One thing noted in the home was a sense of comradeship and admiration for the insight, integrity, and courage of the mother. "Woe to those who call evil good and good evil."

The inversion of values is evident in the euphemisms we encounter daily. Instead of referring to a submarine frankly as an instrument of war, Rear Admiral William Rayburn Jr., boss of the Polaris project, called it: "This new star of peace."[16] The term defense refers to the power designed for attack or retaliation. "Deterrence" is used where "provocation" would be more accurate. "Security" refers to the insecurity our weapons produce. Wishful thinking and the desire to salve one's conscience have obscured the harsh realities.

We are committing what Jesus called the unforgivable sin. We shall scarcely repent of the evil of waging war if we label it "good." Without repentance, we shall not seek forgiveness. Nor shall we dedicate ourselves to the cause of peace if we consider it evil. By inverting the meaning of "right" and "wrong," we become, as Jesus expressed it, "guilty of an eternal sin" (Mark 3:19–30).

LACK
OF EFFECTIVE MORAL RESTRAINTS

A conclusion implied by much of the preceding, but that requires emphasis, is that World War II and plans for World

War III have demonstrated the lack of effective restraints on the war system. By "war system," I refer to preparation for war, the decision to wage war, and to actions engaged in during periods of relative peace, such as interventions and covert operations, as well as conduct during overt warfare. A nation may still abide by international laws prohibiting random, purposeless killing, but when it comes to protecting its vital interests, it is likely, under stress, to recognize no limits. This becomes evident as we observe what actually occurs in the war system and the way alleged "military necessity" takes precedence over moral considerations.

1. *The logic of inhumane practices.* I shall not deal here with the concept of "limited nuclear war," with each side "taking out" only selected enemy targets. This has been effectively refuted elsewhere. An excellent, short treatment is contained in the American Catholic bishops' pastoral letter, *The Challenge of Peace: God's Promise and Our Response.* The footnotes to that discussion contain a bibliography, plus quotations by seven officials who have served at the highest military posts and policy levels of the U.S. government. Their conclusion is that "control would be lost on both sides and the exchange would become unconstrained."[17]

The point I wish to make here is that modern war has become such that no tradition, laws of war, or moral considerations can any longer be relied on to restrain the conduct of major powers. This is because the means of destruction have become so effective that entire nations could be at risk. The stakes have been raised, with the result that defeat could be catastrophic. When the chips are down, a nation will feel pressed to commit any atrocity to avoid defeat—then to hasten the end of the war—then to win a particular battle—then to protect a vital interest. This extension of military necessity is justified, quite logically, by the domino theory. If we do not protect a vital interest, who knows where our neglect might lead?

The atrocities committed during World War II and in

Vietnam simply highlight a characteristic of war per se that has long been recognized. Michael Walzer, in his classic treatment of just-war doctrine, quotes the noted theorist of war, Karl von Clausewitz: "War is an act of force . . . which theoretically can have no limits." After developing Clausewitz' concept, Walzer brings us up to our era with the observation of General Eisenhower: "When you resorted to force . . . you didn't know where you were going. . . . If you got deeper and deeper, there was just no limit except . . . the limitations of force itself."[18]

From a different perspective, some strategists have long contended that the most humane way to conduct a war is to make it as inhumane as possible in order to end it sooner, thus limiting the total number of casualties. War is based on the view that a presumably good end justifies a means that would otherwise be condemned. In discussing the barbarities committed by General Sherman in the U.S. Civil War, historian Geoffrey Best notes that during the early phases of the war, Sherman "yielded to none in his explicit regard for . . . the law of war," which was "often the beacon of his thoughts." He scrupulously distinguished civilians from soldiers. But "his mind gradually changed." The inexorable logic of war drove humane people—Sherman, Grant, and Lincoln—to commit or condone inhumane acts. "What else could they do," asks Best, "unless they were willing to admit defeat?"[19] The following examples show that this was not an exceptional case.

In World War I, Allied soldiers were assigned the task of following an advance and bashing in the heads of dead or wounded German soldiers. This prevented the Germans from "faking it" and then getting up and attacking the Allies from the rear. In the Vietnam war, U.S. soldiers shot women and children who appeared to be noncombatants, but some of whom might otherwise have sniped at them. Shortly before World War II started, I shared a train ride across Germany with Nazi soldiers. I asked how they justified the early-morning blood purge in which Storm Troopers had slaughtered hundreds of civilians. They replied that it was better to kill a

76

few hundred suspected revolutionaries than to let the movement grow until a civil war killed thousands.

During the Korean War, only about half the U.S. infantrymen fired their weapons at advancing enemy soldiers. This was naturally disturbing to Brigadier General S.L.A. Marshall and the Operations Research Office. The problem was traced back to cultural and religious sanctions against killing, to which the soldiers had been exposed since childhood. General Marshall and university psychiatrists set about, with some success, "to remold the human material."[20]

The significance of these incidents is that in each case, the action made sense. It had a purpose. The comment of one writer about the Korean situation provides food for thought:

> As long as military power is our chosen method of national defense, the military authorities are under obligation to be as efficient as possible—to do their utmost to guarantee victory. . . . A child raised in a religious environment must have these "inhibitions" and convictions rooted out before he can become a good soldier. . . . Must we give up our religious and democratic values to wage war? If we do, what is there left to defend?[21]

These episodes are consistent with aspects of U.S. strategy that came to light in 1984. Low intensity warfare—terrorism, hostage-taking, etc.—has been increasing worldwide. In response, a U.S. official contends that if the United States is to protect its interests abroad, it must "have a department of dirty tricks. . . . We should sanction murder as a national policy—tightly controlled and not used very often."[22] Secretary of State George Shultz adds that some innocent people may be killed, "but we cannot become the Hamlet of nations, worrying endlessly over whether and how to respond."[23]

The surfacing of the Central Intelligence Agency (CIA) manual, *Psychological Operations in Guerrilla War*, which advocated "neutralizing" selected officials in Nicaragua, caused a furor; but it simply expressed standard CIA operating procedure. When William Fulbright was chairman of the Senate Foreign Relations Committee, he admitted:

> *There is no point in our pretending that . . . intelligence operations do not . . . involve violations of every Commandment. They do. Lying, cheating, murder, stealing, seduction, and suicide are part of the unpleasant business in which all great nations participate—not because they want to, not because they believe these acts are moral, but because they believe such activities are essential to their own self-preservation.*[24]

I do not contend that moral issues are never raised. Sometimes they are. My point is that the nature of war is such that, especially in modern times, when a nation relies on military force for its defense and security, sooner or later it will probably abandon any constraints that moral scruples would impose.

2. Just-war restraints not effective. The question may be raised whether the excesses of modern war can be effectively limited by application of the just-war criteria, which have guided Roman Catholic thinking for the past sixteen hundred years and which were incorporated into Protestant creeds during the Reformation. Underlying the criteria are two assumptions: that some wars are legitimate and that certain restraints should apply to their conduct. The criteria are to be used in determining which wars are legitimate and what restraints should apply.

Regarding legitimacy, the most relevant criterion for our purpose is that of proportionality: engaging in a given war must reasonably be expected to produce more good than harm—that is, it must prevent more evil than it causes. The standard of proportionality also applies to the conduct of war—the good of a certain method must outweigh the evil. A closely related criterion is that of discrimination: noncombatants must not be killed intentionally and the amount of unintentional killing must not be disproportionate to the good that may reasonably be anticipated. These definitions should suffice for our purpose, although they scarcely do justice to the complex reasoning that has been devoted to this issue over the years. The following discussion will be brief in order to avoid duplicating other treatments of the issue, notably that of John Yoder (see Bibliography).

Some ethicists who formerly used just-war criteria, and who now justify the possible use of nuclear weapons, tend to discard the criteria as obsolete, since the mass killing of civilians would be inevitable in nuclear war and very likely in conventional wars. It would be more consistent and justifiable to apply the criteria and draw the necessary conclusion that modern war (with the possible exception of strictly limited conventional wars) is morally wrong.

The issue is faced with commendable directness by the Alternative Defence Commission in Britain: "The crux of the moral debate is whether the political objective of preventing a possible Soviet occupation would justify waging a nuclear war. The answer from common sense, from . . . just-war theory, and from the whole ethical tradition . . . is that it would not."[25] This brings the consistent just-war theorist closer to the pacifist, who believes that all war is wrong. The narrowing of this gap can be seen in official pronouncements of the Catholic Church, culminating in the American bishops' pastoral letter of 1983.

Considerable hair-splitting occurs when just-war theorists deal with deterrence. If it is wrong to *use* nuclear weapons, is it wrong to *possess* them? To *threaten* their use? To *intend* to use them under circumstances that their possession is meant to prevent? Much of the discussion tends to obscure the real issues rather than to clarify them. The most perceptive conclusions regarding the morality of war are likely to come not from those who are most adept at balancing one nuance against another, but from common people with clear insight who know that it must be wrong to slaughter millions of their fellow human beings. If the reasoning and conclusions in chapter I are sound—if *possessing* and *threatening* increase the likelihood of *using*—then possessing them must also be condemned.

In religious circles, the just-war doctrine has probably fostered awareness that war should not be undertaken lightly and that its conduct should be subject to certain restraints. Much of the opposition to obliteration bombing of cities in World War II was based on the criterion of discrimination. Some selective conscientious objectors during the Vietnam war reflected the reasoning of just-war theorists. They did not oppose all wars, but considered that particular war wrong. Nuclear pacifists have reasoned in similar fashion in opposing nuclear, but not conventional, war.

Although the just-war doctrine has thus influenced some individuals, it has had little or no restraining effect in the halls of power. We did not hesitate to engage in saturation and atomic bombing of civilians in World War II. Pentagon plans for a protracted nuclear war make it clear that we intend to use our weapons.[26] When policymakers pay any attention to just-war teaching, they contend that the particular war at issue is one that is just, and they ignore the restraints on its conduct that the theory would impose. Despite official declarations that seem to imply the contrary, U.S. missiles are still targeted on Soviet cities, with some being held in reserve to vaporize any survivors who may emerge from the rubble.[27] A realistic look at the past and at plans for the future should convince us that we cannot rely on just-war principles to keep us out of war or to limit any war in which we engage.

OPERATION OF THE MORAL LAW

Is not our transgression enormous?—the callous disrespect for human life, the misuse of our stewardship as we pollute ourselves and our natural resources, the attempt to usurp the prerogatives of God, the inversion of moral distinctions, and the lack of moral restraints. Where will this lead?

I believe that a moral law operates in the universe. This implies an objective difference between right and wrong and that we shall reap what we sow. "Though the mills of God grind slowly, they grind exceeding fine."[28] Those who are familiar with Moses, Amos, Isaiah, and Jeremiah can recall their predictions of divine judgment on transgressing nations and the certain fulfillment of those predictions.

In 1746, John Woolman, a New Jersey Quaker of uncommon ethical sensitivity, reflected on the many evils involved in the slave trade: "I saw in these southern provinces so many vices and corruptions increased by this trade and this way of life, that it appeared to me as a dark gloominess hanging over the land; and though now many willingly run into it, yet in future the consequences will be grievous to posterity!"[29] Ten times in the course of his *Journal*, Woolman repeated his foreboding: If the nation did not repent and cease from oppression, the operation of the moral law would "shake terribly the earth." Woolman thereby put his finger on one of the multiple and complex causes of the Civil War. Today, as we increasingly devote time, energy, and money to ever more fiendish ways of mass murder, can we help seeing a "dark gloominess hanging over the land"?

EXPLANATIONS

Now I do not believe that we are immoral monsters. How, then, have we gone wrong? In chapters I and II we examined what may be termed the self-preservation rationale for our military buildup—that it is needed to deter the Soviet threat. It remains to consider two other explanations for our acquiescence in preparation for a war that could result in omnicide—the extinction of the species.

1. Psychological. A psychological explanation is that we have come to our present attitudes and actions by a process so

81

gradual and apparently inevitable that we have failed to realize how evil they are. This is well expressed by Freeman Dyson, who reminisced in the final weeks of World War II:

> *I began to look backward and to ask myself how it happened that I let myself become involved in this crazy game of murder. Since the beginning of the war I had been retreating step by step from one moral position to another, until at the end I had no moral position at all. At the beginning of the war I believed fiercely in the brotherhood of man, called myself a follower of Gandhi, and was morally opposed to all violence. After a year of war I retreated and said, Unfortunately nonviolent resistance against Hitler is impracticable, but I am still morally opposed to bombing. A few years later I said, Unfortunately it seems that bombing is necessary in order to win the war, and so I am willing to go to work for Bomber Command, but I am still morally opposed to bombing cities indiscriminately. After I arrived at Bomber Command I said, Unfortunately it turns out that we are after all bombing cities indiscriminately, but this is morally justified as it is helping to win the war. A year later I said, Unfortunately it seems that our bombing is not really helping to win the war, but at least I am morally justified in working to save the lives of the bomber crews. In the last spring of the war I could no longer find any excuses. . . . I had surrendered one moral principle after another, and in the end it was all for nothing.[30]*

Another psychological factor is that we generally require considerable time to adapt to new situations. Modern methods of warfare are so revolutionary that former approaches to international tensions have become anachronistic. Although we often hear that the nuclear age requires new ideas, our foreign policy continues in the same old channels. Having thought and acted in military terms for centuries, we find it hard to conceive of nonviolent methods of seeking national security.

A further reason for acquiescing in the plans for World War III is that we have not squarely faced current realities. This is due partly to our preoccupation with daily activities, but even more to the mechanism of "denial," which Jerome Frank, Johns Hopkins University psychiatrist, has defined as

82

"dealing with unpleasantness by ignoring it."[31] Our minds tend to switch off disagreeable channels of thought, causing us to postpone dealing with very real dangers.

"Selective inattention" is especially seductive in regard to nuclear war because the dangers are not evident. We do not actually see missiles, submarines, and disease germs, and we lack the imagination fully to realize their reality. When we momentarily perceive our danger it is psychologically attractive to dismiss it with the attitude: "It won't happen to me." To reinforce this attitude, the political, military, and business leaders who have immediate interests in continuing the arms race bombard us with propaganda. To accept their reassuring clichés and unexamined assumptions is easier than to think critically and challenge them.

2. *Defense of freedom.* A more rational justification, with moral overtones, goes something like this: We may not wish to commit the most horrible atrocities, but the readiness for nuclear war is necessary to preserve our liberty. To have our freedom curtailed is unthinkable. Even total destruction, we are told, would be better than living in slavery; we should be willing to die, if necessary, for death is not the worst evil.

This appears reasonable until we examine it more closely. Then we note its false assumptions and serious perversion of values. First, look at the assertion that the loss of life is preferable to the loss of freedom. Whether or not that is true, it obscures the fact that voluntary exposure to death is not a goal of war. The real aim is not to die, but to kill. The ethical difference between being willing to sacrifice one's own life and being ready to kill is expressed sharply by Edna St. Vincent Millay:

I shall die, but that is all that I shall do for Death.
I am not on his pay-roll.[32]

Moreover, a nuclear war will affect not just major powers, but noncombatant nations and future generations as well. In view of its total effects, can we honestly consider nuclear war to be the lesser of two evils?

A favorite phrase of those who justify our military might is "peace with freedom." The result of linking two values this way is that it leaves their relationship ambiguous. It is not clear whether one is meant to imply the other, whether one is considered a prerequisite for the other, or—most important— which is to come first if a choice must be made. In Defense Department statements, for example, the phrase seems to imply that our military strength ensures both peace and freedom. As explained in the earlier chapters, that is a highly dubious assumption. In the nuclear era, to assume that actual war could protect either peace or freedom would be patently false.

Freedom is a noble ideal for which we should strive with unrelenting vigor. It rightly inspires us all. All honor to Mahatma Gandhi, Martin Luther King, and all who struggle for freedom without sacrificing the values of reconciliation, mercy, and love. But when those with special interests speak of freedom, we need to ask several questions about it. Whose freedom do we mean? Freedom for what?

We need to beware lest the ideal becomes an idol— exalted above its proper level to the rank of deity. An idol is not what it appears to be. It is a false god, in which the divine and demonic are intermingled. Those who keep referring to peace with freedom exalt political freedom too highly. Whatever lies behind the slogan, we must not make freedom an idol, for the sake of which, like the ancient worshipers of Moloch, we are ready to sacrifice in the fire our own children—plus ourselves, other people's children, and all humanity.

Our idolization of freedom is illumined by Paul Tillich's distinction between preliminary concerns and ultimate concern. The former may be so noble that they rightfully demand our attention, devotion, and passion. But they should not be given our *"infinite* attention, *unconditional* devotion and *ulti-*

mate passion." They are important but not ultimately so. Yet, declares Tillich, each of these lesser concerns "tries to become our ultimate concern, our god," and we often maintain such a concern as if it were ultimate. He then points out that the most demanding of these idols is the nation.[33] Like motherhood and apple pie, one can scarcely question the value of freedom. It has a strong emotional appeal. But I have the uneasy feeling that it is a cover-up: that we worship national self-interest in the guise of freedom.

Let us think for a moment of genuine freedom for rich and poor alike—in political or physical terms, as it is generally understood. By what twisted process have people with a Judeo-Christian heritage come to assume that freedom is so important that one must give up all moral and spiritual principles—as modern war requires—for its sake? Jesus lived in an occupied nation and repeatedly rejected the temptation to be a military leader who would free his people from the yoke of Rome. What of the early Christians who gave up their freedom and lived in catacombs rather than betray their principles? What of the people throughout history who have relinquished physical freedom by going to jail for their convictions? Were they mistaken? Should they have worshiped the emperor, entered the army, or otherwise pleased the authorities because, after all, "We must have our freedom"? In so acting, would they not have lost the true freedom based on a higher loyalty? This freedom no dictatorship can destroy.

It is extremely doubtful that the only alternatives before us are mass murder or drastic reduction of freedom. Were that the case, however, surely we should choose the latter. If we engage in mass murder, we impair what is of ultimate worth—our moral being. But what others can do to us need not destroy our moral and spiritual selves, unless we let it. The "one thing needed," declares Tillich, is concern about that which is ultimate. Having this passion we can still be concerned about lesser matters, such as freedom and the nation, but in a different way. Our anxiety about these things will be gone, its power broken. If we should lose these things, we do not lose the one thing we need and that cannot be taken from us.[34]

The one thing needed is to do that which is moral. Our present course is immoral. It is one of those ways of living and acting that is so wrong we would be required to abandon it even if we could not foresee just what road to take. Could any alternative be worse than our present acquiescence in mass slaughter? If we have a modicum of belief in a moral or divine order, we have grounds to expect that there must be a better way.

Chapter V.

AN ALTERNATIVE
TO MILITARY DEFENSE

BEFORE EXPLORING a better way of addressing the problem of national security, it should be instructive to look briefly at the values and limitations of violence as a method of seeking justice or defending a nation. At this point, I shall deal more with revolutions within nations than with international war, since the contrast with nonviolent methods can be seen more readily at that level. Similar reasoning may then be applied to international conflicts.

THE NATURE AND EFFECTIVENESS
OF VIOLENCE

Generally, we conceive of violence in terms of obvious methods of inflicting injury on people or damage to property. But violence is often covert or systemic, woven into the very fabric of society. Leo Tolstoy called attention to this in *The Law of Love and the Law of Violence*. Referring to such respected figures as the judge and the landed proprietor, he observed: "We do not perceive all the crimes they commit each day in the name of the public good."[1] This type of violence is so built into the structure of social and political institutions that its agents are scarcely aware of it. It becomes overt when those who hold political and economic power feel threatened. It is then used by the police or the military, ostensibly to preserve law and order.

As for violence used by those who are oppressed, its underlying cause is usually frustration—a sense of deserving a better lot, plus the conviction that little progress is being made toward its attainment. Faced with the frustration of millions of underprivileged people throughout the Third World and with the intransigence of their oppressors, a significant number of religious leaders and theologians have come to sanction violence by the oppressed. They condone it when they believe that the cause is just, a favorable outcome is possible, and no other method will attain the goal. Liberation theologians consider freeing the oppressed to be an imperative of the Christian gospel. To attain this end, some of them condone violent revolution, whereas others sanction only nonviolent methods.

In certain cases and to some extent, violence achieves the aims of its agents. For those who are oppressed, it may serve as an effective means of communication. It may dramatize their condition and force those in power to take their needs seriously. The riots and protests in the United States in the last half of the 1960s stimulated public awareness of conditions in the ghettos and of the determination of blacks to tolerate them no longer.

Moreover, violence sometimes gains its immediate end. Witness the American Revolution. Another example is noted by Hannah Arendt, referring to French student violence in the late 1960s: "France would not have received the most radical reform bill since Napoleon, to change her antiquated education system, without the riots of the French students."[2]

The benefits of violence are not limited to possible changes in the social order. As Jean-Paul Sartre has observed, the participants may gain a sense of personal fulfillment.[3] When the systemic violence of society has for generations beaten down a group of people, they tend to become like things, with little sense of identity or humanity. To react violently can have an energizing and purifying effect; they attain psychological release through purging themselves of fear and giving vent to repressed rage. By rioting, people can sometimes change their environment. For once they count for something. They gain a sense of power, and force the oppressor to recognize them as persons. They become liberated from thinghood. In saying "No" to the oppressor, they affirm their dignity as people with free choice. They are saying "Yes" to their essential being.

A feeling of group unity may also be experienced. In Erich Maria Remarque's *All Quiet on the Western Front*, one senses the comradeship felt by soldiers in the trenches. Likewise, participants in a riot or revolution may feel a new sense of belonging to a community as they join forces in a common cause. Even suffering together gives meaning to a previously humdrum existence. Further, intense activity conveys a sense of movement that attracts others to the group.

THE INADEQUACY OF VIOLENCE

Genuine as these benefits of violence are, they constitute only part of the picture. The same benefits could generally be obtained by nonviolent methods. The sit-ins and bus boycotts by the blacks communicated and dramatized their needs more effectively than did the riots. The participants in nonviolent actions gained a sense of fulfillment and emotional release fully as energizing as violent activists experienced. Bonds of comradeship and group unity were also forged by their common struggles and sufferings.

In civil conflicts, the harm done by violence almost always outweighs the good. Studies by experts in different fields agree that while violence may change the situation, it seldom improves it and generally makes it worse—whether it is the action of government against dissidents or vice versa.[4] The government "wins" more often than the dissidents, but the benefits are usually short-lived. Trouble breaks out again unless the causes of the original grievances are remedied. When the dissidents win, the end result is seldom better, even from the standpoints of those who support the violence. Whichever side wins, many characteristics of a police state are likely to emerge. The government adopts repressive measures to prevent further revolts, or the successful dissidents do so to restrain counter-revolutionaries. Insofar as "law and order" are achieved by either party, it is by way of totalitarianism.

Reason also becomes a casualty. The emotions of fear and hostility gain the ascendancy. Members of the group against which violence is directed become alarmed at the threat to their privileges and identities. They respond with more rigid and savage resistance. "I just went animal," exclaimed a policeman to University of Michigan sociologist Albert Reiss during an investigation of the Newark, New Jersey riot of 1967. Even more violent revolts may follow. As the escalating conflict becomes prolonged or renewed, each side tends to develop a basically irrational ideology solidifying its attitude.

A pervasive effect of violence is that it sets a precedent and example that leads to further violence. It was no accident that the violent aspects of the black power movement emerged during the Vietnam war. The carnage engaged in by U.S. forces in Vietnam gave oppressed groups in our society cause to feel justified in resorting to lesser degrees of violence to rectify greater injustices. If one can kill for the nation, why not kill for a better Harlem? The power of precedent is even more insidious in causing violence to become acclimated into our mores. The temper of our thinking gradually changes; acts that once filled us with horror become acceptable. Taboos against killing diminish, and respect for human life becomes a casualty of the process.

Despite its short-term effectiveness on some occasions, I believe that, on balance, resort to violence is counterproductive. In the preceding paragraphs, I have dealt primarily with internal strife, where violence is more likely to seem justifiable. In the international sphere, the tendency for violence to escalate portends global disaster. This means that the chain of

90

violence must be broken. We must find an alternative method of providing for national defense.

A POSSIBLE ALTERNATIVE: CIVILIAN-BASED DEFENSE

A statement often made by government spokespersons is that nuclear weapons cannot be disinvented; even if they are all dismantled, the knowledge of how to build them will remain. Therefore, they contend, we shall always need a strong military defense to deter a potential enemy or to fight a war if deterrence fails. We shall need to retain nuclear weapons or the readiness to build them.

From the same facts, I draw the opposite conclusion. In the latter part of chapter III, I expressed the view that a broad consensus is developing that if we want to survive, we must change our course. I noted that several able individuals and groups have made practical proposals for reducing our weaponry in order to produce a safer world. I agree with the near-term agenda set by these proposals. My concern about most of them, however, is that they are not far-reaching enough to provide long-term security. They rely basically on military power for national defense. In the case of an accident, crisis, or aggressor, this reliance could lead to war. And because building weapons of mass destruction will always be possible, any major prolonged war could be so catastrophic that it must be avoided at all costs. Faced with this peril—unprecedented in human history—the only rational choice is to respond in a way that is also unprecedented.

Whether we approach the issue from a moral, biblical, or practical perspective, it seems to me that we must come up with the same answer: Eventually we need to abandon war as our method of defense. Naturally, some of us may recoil at such a suggestion. Unaware of any other method, we may become anxious at the prospect of being unprotected. This concern is legitimate; we should be able to defend our country. Now comes the good news! There is a new approach to our new situation. We may be able to develop a sound alternative to military defense. Obviously, this cannot be accomplished overnight. It would be preceded by a drastic reduction of nuclear weapons and by other aspects of the approach to foreign policy advocated in chapter III. As mentioned there, it would be reinforced by establishment of the conditions necessary for an enduring peace. It will come about only after, working with other nations, we have alleviated the causes of war, reduced the worldwide level of violence, and created a favorable atmosphere. It will doubtless be years—probably decades—before we will be willing and able to take this radical step, but I believe that eventually we must do it if we are to preserve our cherished values.

I refer to a method that is generally called "civilian-based defense" (CBD) because it relies on the population as a whole instead of a special category of armed forces. It consists of engaging in active nonviolent resistance if an attempt is made to conquer and occupy a country. In a sense, this method is not new or without precedent. It has been used at various times and places for different purposes. Best known is its use under Gandhi's leadership to achieve independence for India; under the leadership of Martin Luther King in the struggle for civil rights; and by the Solidarity movement in contemporary Poland. Not so well known, but quite significant, was the success of nonviolent methods of resistance to Hitler in the Netherlands, Denmark, and Norway during World War II.

Civilian-based defense is new in the sense that it has not been officially adopted by any nation as its only, or primary, method of defense. Nor has it been advocated by many avid workers for peace. After criticizing our present military buildup and shortsighted foreign policy, they are likely to remark, "Of course, I favor a strong national (meaning 'military') defense."

One reason that nonviolent defense has scarcely been considered, until recently, is that people in general have inadequate conceptions of what it would involve. To many it connotes simply passive submission to aggression. Actually, it would be quite different. It involves a type of direct action that has proved remarkably effective. While rejecting violence, it is active rather than passive and entails resistance rather than submission. Martin Luther King called this method a "higher synthesis." It avoids killing but actively opposes the adversary. As a method of national defense, it would have the potential to resolve the dilemma of those who would be strongly impelled to active resistance but who could not conscientiously use violence.

Nonviolent resistance that would be used by CBD requires careful, disciplined planning, preparation, and organization, as well as strong commitment to the goal and pacific methods of attaining it. The techniques used vary according to the circumstances. At the simplest level, it involves vigorous protest and attempts at persuasion—such as dialogue with the opponents, petitions, marches, and picketing. While this raises the issue, it must usually be followed by the next level: noncooperation—the withholding of support by such means as strikes, boycotts, and the refusal to obey orders. A final step is intervention—directly impeding the functioning of the opponent. Typical methods include sit-ins, blocking the path of tanks, even acts of sabotage when no human lives are at risk. Considerable pressure is sometimes exerted—what King called "constructive coercive power."

The power of nonviolence is wielded by the citizens of a country. Those who would rule depend on the cooperation and assistance, or at least the submission and obedience, of the population. Their power evaporates if enough people withhold their support—even in the face of threats or death. People may not realize that they have this power, or they may lack the consensus, courage, or persistence to exercise it. But when they do, the would-be rulers must take it into account. This was evident in Iran in 1979, when the masses persistently demanded the abdication of the shah. People power in the Philippines forced the ouster of Ferdinand Marcos in 1986. The military might of the dictators was unavailing.

The line between violent and nonviolent resistance cannot always be sharply drawn. Critics might object that Martin Luther King's "coercive power" is scarcely distinguishable from milder forms of violence. One might cavil endlessly and imagine hypothetical situations in which the nonviolent resister could hardly be 100 percent consistent. All this may be granted; in our complex world, one can seldom be an absolutist. Yet there is a basic qualitative difference between military and nonviolent defense. The crucial question is whether the shift could be made from one to the other, a process referred to as transarmament, which is the focus of the Association for Transarmament Studies. Initially, the two methods might be components of a nation's total defense strategy. Both were used successfully in thwarting the Nazi occupation forces in Denmark in World War II. In recent years, the Swedish Ministry of Defense has been engaged in strategy studies exploring a combination of both methods of resisting an aggressor.

The governments of Norway and the Netherlands have also sponsored studies of the feasibility of nonviolent defense. It has been adopted as official policy by the Green party in West Germany. Exclusive reliance on it by any of these countries would probably be preceded by a combination of military and nonmilitary defense. The former could be phased out gradually as confidence in the latter increased.

Before proceeding further, let us explore the extent to which nonviolent defense may be expected to achieve certain goals. In previous chapters, I examined three functions of military power in implementing U.S. foreign policy. One is to deter the alleged Soviet threat, which takes three forms: to conquer and occupy the United States or Western Europe, to bomb us into oblivion, and to encroach on our vital interests. A second function of military power is to protect our interests and expand our spheres of influence throughout the world. The third is to fight and win wars.

It seems clear that replacing military might with non-violent methods of defense would effectively remove the threat of the Soviet Union bombing us into oblivion, since it is our threat to them that would provide the incentive for them to strike first. As far as protecting our interests abroad is concerned, military action does not serve us well, and insofar as it is effective, it generally benefits only a small elite segment of the population. It too often means supporting the exploitation of the people and natural resources of other countries. Instead of risking war to protect our access to Middle East oil, we would do better to become more self-sufficient through conserving our own resources and developing alternative sources of energy. The best long-term approach to countering the threat or encroachment on our vital interests lies in developing better relations with the Soviet Union and Third World nations.

Yet a realistic approach compels us to recognize that giving up our military threat and becoming vulnerable to threats by others would entail some economic loss. It would involve the reduction of foreign operations and the profits gained thereby. Such economic loss would be more than offset, however, by the enormous savings brought on by the shift from military to nonviolent methods of defense. Reliance on CBD would also have the tremendous advantage of keeping us from getting into a nuclear war by way of military confrontation abroad. In particular, pulling our soldiers out of Europe would serve to reduce tension there, especially if our allies also eliminated their offensive threat. From both practical and ethical perspectives, the net effect of CBD, while entailing some disadvantages, would be beneficial to our legitimate interests. The world would be a safer place.

Concerning the third function of our military power—to fight and win wars—CBD would require abandoning that aspect of our foreign policy. But we should abandon it anyway. In what follows, I shall deal with the ethical basis and practical effectiveness of CBD. This is relevant to the remaining Soviet threat mentioned earlier—to conquer Western Europe or the United States, which I examined in chapter II. I am thinking now of its broader application as a substitute for the main function of the armed forces—to defend a nation against attack. The issue concerns transarmament—replacing the whole war system with CBD.

ETHICAL BASIS
AND PRACTICAL EFFECTIVENESS
OF CBD

My purpose here is not to delve into the detailed history and methods of active nonviolent resistance, which could be used for CBD. This has been done thoroughly in the sources listed in the Bibliography. My aim, rather, is to stress the significance of CBD, raise our level of awareness regarding it, and contribute to making it a matter of national debate. The Catholic bishops' pastoral letter on war and peace expresses my conviction: "Practical reason as well as spiritual faith demands that it [nonviolent defense] be given serious consideration as an alternative course of action."[5]

1. Military defense neither moral nor practical. In examining the moral and practical aspects of CBD, we need to keep the alternative clearly before us. Even before weapons of mass destruction were developed, war was hardly a moral pursuit. The best that could be claimed for it was that in some instances, it may have been the lesser evil. As for its practicality, it must be rated well below 50 percent. When a nation resorts to arms, it almost invariably assumes it will win. Yet victory is not attained by more than half the belligerents. For every winner there is a loser. The losing nation does not accomplish its objectives. Even the victor seldom gains all it sought, and against the gains must be balanced the loss of life, destruction of cities, disruption of the economy, and other costs of war. Moreover, the conflict usually plants the seeds of hatred and revenge that produce another war. In our day, the balance weighs even more heavily against war. It could scarcely be considered moral or practical if it destroys the belligerent nations as well as millions of civilians in noncombatant nations.

Critics of nonviolent resistance often assume that if it does not always accomplish its objectives, or if it has any disadvantages, it is thereby discredited. Surely its advocates do not contend that it never entails cost or sacrifice. Nor do they expect it always to achieve its goals. But to discard it for these reasons would be to commit what logicians term the "fallacy of objections." When two positions are being compared, objections to one of them discredit it only if they are more basic than the objections to its alternative.[6] In deciding which position is superior, we must take into account all the merits and faults of each. No matter how impractical nonviolent resistance may be, it cannot be as impractical as war.

We must remember also that if nonviolent defense would not be as effective as we might wish, the fault may lie with the legacy left by the war system, rather than with the new approach. A nation with a heritage of war, fear, and mistrust might be attacked by an adversary if it suddenly shifted to nonviolent defense. Of course, such a change would not occur suddenly; a long gradual period of preparation would have preceded it. In any case, if we are ever to break the chain of circumstances that cause wars, we must begin sometime. As a nation gradually builds up a heritage of peace, the practicality of nonviolence would become more evident.

2. Ethical basis for CBD. Nonviolent methods may be used simply as techniques to accomplish certain goals. They do not depend on particular religious or philosophical convictions. Such leaders as King and Gandhi, however, conceived of their movements as being grounded in a sound philosophy, including faith "in the ultimate morality of the universe . . . that all reality hinges on moral foundations."[7] This faith was well expressed by John Ruskin, who had a strong influence on Gandhi:

97

*Not one of us . . . can ever know what the result of these
actions . . . will be for ourselves or for others. But we all can
know which action is just and which is not. We can know also
that the consequences of justice will, eventually, be as good as
possible, for others as for ourselves, although we can never
say of what this good will consist.*[8]

Ruskin's view is reflected by George Kennan, whose experience led him to conclude that one cannot accurately predict the consequences of a decision regarding foreign policy; they seldom coincide fully with what is intended. Therefore, he maintained, we should be especially concerned to use ethical means, which will be more conducive to good ends than will strategic calculation with little regard to the ethical quality of the means.[9]

Gandhi attributed our inability to calculate precisely the means-end relationship to our being instruments of an Almighty Will rather than arbiters of our own destinies. This led him to concentrate on the purity of the means and to consider adherence to truth and enhancement of human personality more important than the attainment of specific ends. Martin Luther King emphasized the coherence of means and ends: the means represent the end in process. As in the relationship of the tree to the seed, the end is preexistent in the means. Hence an evil means cannot produce a good end.

Closely related to this view of the means-end relationship is a strong belief in the imperative of duty and its implications. This is the conviction that a person has the unconditional obligation to do what is right and to refrain from doing what is wrong. There is a certain way of living that one *ought* to pursue. Crucial to this conception is what the philosopher Kant called a "good will," which "is not good because of what it effects or accomplishes . . . ; it is good only because of its willing, i.e., it is good of itself." Even if it could achieve nothing of its purpose, "it would sparkle like a jewel in its own right, as something that had its full worth in itself."[10] Not all advocates of nonviolence agree with Kant to the same extent, but for the most part they conceive nonviolent resistance to be the expression of such an imperative. Many of them share the conviction that because of its accord with the moral nature of the universe, it is more likely than violence to succeed.

An integral aspect of the philosophies of Kant and Gandhi is commitment to the realization of truth. This led Gandhi to be ever receptive to the suggestions of his opponents. Respect for truth was basic in his campaigns and made him impregnable in conducting them. Christians like Thomas Merton have likewise found stability and inner power in the confidence that truth is invincible because Jesus Christ, "the Lord of truth, is indeed risen and reigning over his Kingdom, defending the deepest values of those who dwell in it."[11]

Truth is one of the casualties of the war system. Operatives of the Central Intelligence Agency could not fulfill their functions if they were committed to truth. Government officials would find it harder to prepare for war, or conduct it, if they did not deceive the public; the inversion of moral distinctions described in chapter IV is a case in point.

In addition to conceptions of the harmony of means and ends, the moral imperative, and the significance of truth, several further convictions, in varying degrees, are held by advocates of nonviolent resistance. One that underlies many of the others is that human life and personality are sacred. To kill people or treat them as things is wrong. For those who have a religious orientation, this is implied in the belief that people are children of God, who must be treated as such. In this respect, nonviolent defense would avoid the most immoral aspect of war depicted in chapter IV—disregarding the sanctity of human life.

According to this view, the respect that is due to human life and personality applies to all people. Humankind is regarded as essentially one. Insofar as a method sets group against group, or person against person, it is wrong. People must not be polarized into opposite camps. Because the aggressor and the defender are not inherently different, reconciliation is a feasible, ultimate objective. This belief in the basic unity of all people renders more acceptable what in any case is inevitable—that since we share the same planet with the Soviets, we must learn to live together.

Beyond this is the conviction that we are meant to love one another. Whereas violence seeks the good of only one contending party, nonviolent direct action, if guided by love, seeks the welfare of all. Love is viewed not as a limitation, but as a dynamic force to aid in solving the basic issues by overcoming the fears and hatreds of the contending parties. This has been well expressed by Robert E. Fitch:

> One thing above all else we have to do right now, and that is to seek out the true sources of our being, whether as children of God or as children of Satan. In the hands of every person . . . lie two great powers. One is the power to love, the other is the power to hate. Almost limitless are the destruction and disruption any individual can work when . . . moved by hate. But equally limitless are the health and creativity one can call forth in oneself and others when . . . moved by love.[12]

Gandhi and King believed that when one makes a decision on ethical grounds, such as to reject violence, added insight, power, and creativity are gained for the employment of appropriate methods. When Gandhi was asked what nonviolent plan he had to prevent World War II, he replied:

> I have no ready-made concrete plan. For me too this is a new field. Only I have no choice as to the means. It must always be purely nonviolent, whether I am closeted with the members of the working committee or with the viceroy. Therefore what I am doing is itself part of the concrete plan. More will be revealed to me from day to day, as all my plans always have been.[13]

This is akin to the Christian faith that after a radical moral decision is made, further light is granted and the decision validated. In this way, such an ethical basis for a nonviolent defense system, although not essential to its practical effectiveness, would probably contribute to it.

100

3. Practical effectiveness of nonviolent resistance. One obvious advantage of the nonviolent approach is that its success does not depend on superior physical force. It has power of its own, which is probably enhanced by an ethical component—the sense of being in the right, not only in reference to goals, but also in the use of means. This creates an esprit de corps that is conducive to steadfastness and reliability. Moreover, it tends to gain the approval of third parties—those who are not yet committed but whose eventual support may be crucial.

Nonviolent action also facilitates a more intelligent choice of objectives. It can have clear, specific goals, while maintaining sufficient flexibility to change or modify them for sound reasons. The goals of warring parties are more likely to reflect emotional, rather than rational, factors. Hence they are less likely to be well defined or subject to judicious modification. They often undergo change in the stress of combat, but such changes are likely to be for the worse; even victory may be followed by chaos, in which dissident factions struggle for power and the incumbents exercise ruthless suppression.

Another merit of nonviolence is that it clarifies the moral distinction between the aggressor, who is using violence, and the defender, who is not. When both sides are violent, each rationalizes its own position and has grounds for accusing the opponent, so that any moral distinctions become veiled in obscurity. If the defender wins, the aggressor continues to feel self-righteous and hostile. The conflict has sown the seeds of future discord. Milton has stated this distinction well: "Who overcomes by force hath overcome but half his foe."

The refusal to use violence constitutes, in effect, an appeal to the moral sensitivities of the aggressors; unable to accuse the defenders, they are more likely to confront their own practice and see its invalidity. Facing opponents who are willing to endure unmerited suffering without retaliating, the aggressors find themselves in an unexpected situation in which their morale for fighting is undercut. As their fear, anxiety, and hostility are reduced, they may come to feel respect and sympathy for the sufferer. This opens the way for union and the cooperation needed not only to handle immediate problems, but also to minimize future conflicts and deal with them effectively.

Bearing these advantages in mind, we may ask whether the people of Western Europe or the United States would adopt and adhere to a nonviolent method of defense and whether it would be successful if they did. The question may be raised whether violence is so deeply rooted in our being as to make such a defense impossible. Books have been written supporting each side of this controversy about human nature. No one denies, however, that people have been able to live peaceably together, so that the question is largely irrelevant. Nonviolent methods of conflict resolution have been taught successfully. Even when strongly provoked, participants in the sit-ins and freedom rides of the civil rights movement in the United States remained nonviolent. Social skills can be learned when the motivation is adequate.

Increasing numbers of people have become aware that the military escalation presumably intended for defense is impelling us to catastrophe. Hence the strong movement to reduce the level of arsenals. Many people are now coming to realize that in view of the destructiveness of modern weapons, even reduction is not enough. They acquiesce in military defense only because they see no alternative.

The purpose of this chapter is to show that Kenneth Boulding was right in declaring: "What is most urgent is that nonviolence should be taken seriously." In his volume *Stable Peace* and other writings, Boulding argues persuasively that in the larger process of societal evolution, areas of stable peace have been expanding. Beginning in Scandinavia after the Napoleonic Wars, as national defense became increasingly costly and useless, this development gained impetus with the advent of nuclear weapons. As Boulding notes, the process does not depend on nonviolent defense. But the adoption of such a defense by smaller nations and its espousal by a few political leaders here just might bring about what Boulding sees as a "profound . . . shift in the nature of the system which carries us . . . over a kind of watershed into a very different social landscape. . . . Where an institution is ripe for delegitimation, a single person, such as Martin Luther King, can have an enormous impact."[14] Recognizing this possibility should provide an antidote to the despair that facing the reality of our peril so often induces.

As noted earlier in regard to the Third World, it may appear that nonviolent resistance has been tried and found wanting. To be sure, methods other than violence have been more or less ineffectual at various times. These include passive submission, attempts at persuasion, protests and demonstrations unrelated to a larger plan, and simple appeals to conscience. Moreover, even campaigns that are carefully planned and conducted may fail. When compared with the success rate of violence, however, nonviolent action fares rather well. A survey of the contemporary world scene scarcely indicates that violent methods are notably successful. The outcome of nonviolent campaigns is often relatively good, even when participants lack able leadership and are neither thoroughly committed to nonviolence nor adequately trained in appropriate behavior and techniques.[15]

The nonviolent (satyagraha) campaigns led by Gandhi produced results not previously considered possible either by opponents or detached observers.[16] The movement in which King was a leader stimulated legislatures, courts, and administrative agencies to remove innumerable legal props for segregation and discrimination. King's untimely death retarded progress and much remains to be done. Yet a great deal was accomplished in a comparatively short time, particularly in regard to education, public facilities, and extending the voting franchise.[17]

A sufficient background of experience is lacking by which to evaluate definitively the potential effectiveness of nonviolent sanctions in CBD against a foreign aggressor. That they hold promise of success is evidenced by the case studies described in the sources listed in the Bibliography. Especially significant are the works of Gene Sharp, of the Center for International Affairs of Harvard University. His two books published in 1985, *National Security Through Civilian-Based Defense* and *Making Europe Unconquerable*, apply to the contemporary world scene the insights gained during a quarter century of study and experience in many countries. Experts in political science, psychology, sociology, anthropology, and other disciplines have added to our knowledge of this alternative.

It is often asserted that the methods of Gandhi and King were effective only because they were dealing with British and Americans, whose reactions reflected relatively humane cultural and religious standards. The question is raised whether nonviolent resistance would work against Nazis, Communists, or others from whom a brutal response might be expected. One could scarcely deny the impact of sociological conditioning and psychological brainwashing. From my own (perhaps biased) perspective, it would seem that a Judeo-Christian heritage would be more conducive to humane conduct than would a society in which atheism was officially promoted. Yet I believe that all human beings have a moral sense. Intense experiences expose qualities that are not ordinarily evident. Armed combat releases sadistic tendencies, and confrontation with voluntary suffering elicits moral sensitivity.

In war and tense situations where the stakes are high, whether the British and Americans act in more humane fashion than Nazis and Communists is open to question. The conduct of people under stress depends not on their ethnic nature or national affiliation. It depends, rather, on such factors as their training, the expectations of their associates (especially those of higher rank), the situation in which they are placed, and whether they believe, for example, that a good end justifies the means considered necessary to achieve it. From this perspective, one can understand why humane people commit inhumane deeds. The Germans and Japanese today, whom we rightly perceive as our friends, are not basically different from our German and Japanese enemies of World War II. We may gain further understanding by reflecting on some of the actions and attitudes of the British and Americans, on the one hand, and those of Nazis and Communists, on the other.

British reactions to the nonviolent independence movement in India are recounted in the biography of Abdul Khaffar Khan by Eknath Easwaran, a native Indian who came to the United States on a Fulbright exchange program. Khan, now more than ninety years old, lived in the Northwest Frontier Province of India, an area inhabited by an ethnic group known as Pathans. Easwaran describes the ruthlessness of the British: "Pathans had to endure mass shooting, torture, the destruction of their fields and homes, jail, flogging, and humiliations." On April 23, 1930, a large crowd of Pathans gathered to protest the arrests of their leaders. Without warning, British troops drove armored cars into the crowd "at great speed." When the villagers remained to collect the dead and wounded, the soldiers opened fire, slaughtering some 250 of them. Easwaran concludes: "The impression that the British were fair and easygoing opponents in India is based largely upon the ignorance in which the treatment of Khan and his people has been shrouded."[18]

As for Americans, evidence of U.S. atrocities in World War II and Vietnam indicate that we, too, can be ruthless. Many of the brutal deeds committed by our armed forces in Vietnam were completely gratuitous, such as dumping an old man into a well and tossing a grenade in after him.[19] More purposive, but still unjustified by any ethical standard, was the massacre of civilians by the saturation bombing of cities in World War II. It was rationalized as helping to bring the war to an end. The aim was to inflict "intense suffering" on civilians in order to so reduce morale through "fear of death or injury for themselves and their loved ones—that they would . . . force their government to capitulate."[20] Senior U.S. weapons scientists also contemplated trying to kill hundreds of thousands of Germans and Japanese by poisoning their food supplies.[21] To dispel any doubt about the readiness of Americans to inflict suffering, one need only ponder a poll taken in 1984. By a vote of 63 percent to 22 percent, Americans favored retaliation to a Soviet nuclear attack "even though it may result in the total destruction of both countries."[22]

Concerning nonviolent resistance to the Nazis, its effectiveness in the occupied countries during World War II is quite instructive. The refusal of the Norwegian teachers to submit to the Nazi authorities was remarkably effective. "You teachers have destroyed everything for us!" fumed an angry Vidkun Quisling (the Norwegian Nazi installed as Minister-President of Norway by the Germans).[23] In France, Pastor André Trocmé inspired the villagers of Le Chambon to adopt nonviolent attitudes and methods in dealing with Nazi officials. This enabled them to hide and smuggle to Switzerland many Jews who would otherwise have been sent to the gas chambers.

After the war, military historian B.H. Liddell Hart interviewed German generals to learn their views on the different kinds of resistance they encountered in Holland, Belgium, and Denmark, as well as in France and Norway. They responded that nonviolence was harder to deal with than violence. This was primarily because they did not know how to cope with it, in contrast to violence, which they were trained to handle.[24] Bad as Hitler was, he was forced to rescind some of his oppressive orders when subordinates could not or would not carry them out.

It should be recognized also that Nazism did not arise in a vacuum. As I observed while studying in Germany in 1931–32, Hitler came to power only because the German people felt humiliated and economically strangled by the war guilt and other provisions of the Versailles Treaty. The refusal of the Allies to accommodate the moderate economic proposals of Hitler's predecessor, Chancellor Bruening, caused a significant proportion of the German people to support Hitler as one who promised to rectify the situation. By the time a major power would have undergone the transformation required to rely on nonviolent defense, it would have adopted a foreign policy that would not produce the frustration on which Hitlerism feeds.

The effectiveness of nonviolent resistance to Communists has been demonstrated on several occasions since World War II. Because thorough accounts appear elsewhere, I shall refer only briefly to a few of them. In 1953, workers in East Germany called a general strike to protest an increase in the work norm decreed by government officials. Under the circumstances, this amounted to a call for a revolution. Widespread throughout East Germany, the rebellion was predominantly nonviolent. This inhibited government officials from repressing it by force. Although the revolt failed to remove the regime, it accomplished its immediate objective—cancellation of the order to increase the workload.[25]

The nonviolent resistance of Czechoslovakians to the Soviet invasion in 1968 was a dramatic instance of the effectiveness of such a method. Had the Czechs attempted violent opposition, they would doubtless have been quashed within a few days, and the invading forces would have been more brutal. As it was, the Soviet Union required eight months to gain control of the nation.[26]

The Solidarity movement in Poland provides further evidence that nonviolent methods can affect the Soviet power structure. The movement has gone underground, and some of its earlier gains have been lost, but censorship has been relaxed, university students have more flexibility in their programs, workers now have greater safety in the workplace, and they have the right to strike and form non-state trade unions.[27]

These experiences in Communist nations show that the police, military officers, and government officials are human beings, some of whom, at great personal risk, joined the rebels, and many of whom simply refrained from decisive action against them. Debates in the politburo during those times of tension provide evidence that the party leadership was not monolithic; different points of view were freely expressed. Theodore Ebert, a German political scientist who made a thorough study of these instances, has concluded: "Large scale nonviolent resistance can be damaging to the ideological confidence of a Communist regime. . . . Historical experience cannot be said to prove that civilian defense against a Communist occupation is bound to fail."[28]

A further question is whether only people who are especially pacific because of religious training or sociological conditioning can remain nonviolent in the struggle for justice when opposed by ruthless oppressors. The answer emerges by looking again at the Muslim Pathans, aptly described as "one of the world's most violent peoples." For centuries the cult of revenge and violence has permeated Pathan society. In defending their homelands and perpetuating their tribal feuds, "Pathan life and history were awash in blood." Yet Abdul Khaffar Khan, inspired by Gandhi, raised an "army" of more than 100,000 Pathans, who remained nonviolent in the face of beatings and killings inflicted by the British in northwest India. They "stirred the whole Indian subcontinent when they put down their daggers and handmade rifles and faced, without retaliating, the worst the armies of a baffled, panicking empire could deal out. It was severe in the extreme."[29] Many other examples confirm that with the proper inspiration and training, even the most violence-prone people can keep their resistance nonviolent in the face of provocation.

We should not infer too much from these cases. They are not entirely analogous to the situation of the United States today. Yet certain of their aspects would be quite relevant to a comprehensive U.S. policy. The range of historical experience on which one can draw in exploring the issue has been expressed by Gene Sharp:

A vast history exists of people who, refusing to be convinced that the apparent "powers that be" were omnipotent, defied and resisted powerful rulers, foreign conquerors, domestic tyrants, oppressive systems, internal usurpers, and economic masters. Contrary to usual perceptions, these means of struggle by protest, noncooperation, and disruptive intervention have played major historical roles in all parts of the world.[30]

Without question, for a nation to rely on such methods would involve risks, dangers, and possible suffering. Our task, however, is not to compare nonviolence with some desirable ideal, but with the probable consequences, risks, and dangers of violence. Even if the two were about equal from the practical standpoint, nonviolence would be preferable on moral grounds. But also in terms of producing favorable and lasting results, nonviolent resistance holds greater promise.

Considering the long sad history of violence and the relative effectiveness of active nonviolent resistance, one must conclude not that it has been tried and found wanting, but that it has been surprisingly successful when tried. Thomas C. Schelling, of Harvard University, summarizes its practical importance: "The potential of nonviolence is enormous. . . . In the end it could be as important as nuclear fission. Like nuclear fission it has implications for peace, war, stability . . . and international and domestic politics."[31]

The conclusion is evident. We must use all available resources to achieve constructive solutions to world problems—to minimize the frustrations that cause war. We must do everything possible to halt the momentum toward destruction and take the steps urgently needed to make the world a safer place in the years immediately ahead. We must develop a method of national defense that will be innovative enough for the nuclear age and provide maximum security for the long term.

A tremendous amount of time, energy, and money is spent trying to achieve security by methods that have always failed in the past and that bring us ever closer to a war that would be murderous and suicidal. It is incomprehensible that so little attention has been given by the major powers, especially the United States, to exploring the feasibility of a nonviolent alternative. Our urgent need now is to consider it seriously. To set our course toward the abandonment of the nuclear arms race in favor of nonviolent national defense would release energies here and abroad that would greatly increase our national security and enhance the quality of life throughout the world.

NOTES

Chapter I.
Deterrence Does Not Work—Strength Brings War

1. *Annual Report to the Congress: Fiscal Year 1984* (Washington, DC: Government Printing Office, 1983), p. 51.

2. Ibid. See also pp. 16, 17, 19, 31–35, 41, and 52.

3. Henry Kissinger, *The Necessity for Choice* (New York: Harper & Row, 1960), pp. 32, 35, 37–38.

4. "Can Nuclear Deterrence Last Out the Century?" *Foreign Affairs*, January 1973, p. 260.

5. Karen E. House, "Haig Cites Evidence . . . ," *Wall Street Journal*, September 14, 1981, p. 2. Although the Germans would presumably be responding to an attack instead of initiating it, the case is relevant, since Haig was assuming that other values would take precedence over survival.

6. See Bruce M. Russett, *No Clear and Present Danger: A Skeptical View of the U.S. Entry into World War II* (New York: Harper & Row, 1972), chap. 3.

7. Robert F. Kennedy, *Thirteen Days: A Memoir of the Cuban Missile Crisis* (New York: New American Library, 1969), pp. 49–50. Cf. Jerome H. Kahan and Anne K. Long, "The Cuban Missile Crisis: A Study of Its Strategic Context," *Political Science Quarterly* 87 (December 1972):573n, 583n.

8. "Sub Dedicated," *Ann Arbor News*, November 12, 1981.

9. Fred H. Wright, "The $18 Billion-a-year Hypothesis," *Fellowship*, April/May 1978, pp. 7–9. Using the American Psychological Association's retrieval system, Wright secured existing psychological research data, from which he concluded: "The higher the threat level . . . the more irrational behavior becomes." Cf. M. Deutsch, "Some Considerations Relevant to National Policy," *Journal of Social Issues* 17 (1961):64. Deutsch analyzes historical experience and concludes that individuals and states are more likely to behave irrationally in a crisis.

10. Kennedy, pp. 44, 31.

11. Henry Muller, "Disarming Threat to Stability," *Time*, November 30, 1981, p. 46.

12. "The Deterrence Deadlock: Is There a Way Out?" Unpublished address given at the Fifth Annual Scientific Meeting, the International Society of Political Psychology, Washington, DC, June 1982, pp. 17, 18.

13. U.S. Congress, Senate, Committee on Armed Services, *Recent False Alerts from the Nation's Missile Attack Warning System: Report of Senators G. Hart and B. Goldwater*, October 9, 1980 (Washington, DC: Government Printing Office, 1980).

14. "Risks of Unintentional Nuclear War: An Overview" and "Computer System Reliability and Nuclear War," *IPPNW Report*, October 1984, pp. 15–21.

15. William Perry, "Why I Quit My Job," *Ethics and Policy*, Special Issue, 1983 (published by the Center for Ethics and Social Policy, Graduate Theological Union, Berkeley, CA), pp. 6–7, 13–14.

16. U.S. Congress, Senate, Committee on Foreign Relations, *Hearings on the Foreign Policy and Arms Control Implications of President Reagan's Strategic Weapons Proposals*, Pt. 1, 97th Cong., 1st sess., November 3, 4, and 9, 1981, p. 110 (Washington, DC: Government Printing Office, 1981).

17. Thomas Schelling, *The Strategy of Conflict* (Cam-

bridge, MA: Harvard University Press, 1960), quoted in Jonathan Schell, "The Fate of the Earth," *New Yorker*, February 15, 1982, p. 61.

18. Experts differ concerning the relative weight to be given to the several possible reasons for dropping the two atom bombs. Nor is there universal agreement regarding whether their use saved lives. At any rate, using the bombs was not a desperate effort to avert defeat. Whether or not the war could have been ended sooner had the United States not insisted on unconditional surrender, it was clear that we would win the war. Victory was within our grasp.

19. E. P. Thompson and Dan Smith, eds., *Protest and Survive* (New York and London: Monthly Review Press, 1981), Introduction by Daniel Ellsberg. The notes to this Introduction contain numerous quotations from several sources concerning these threats.

20. "Two Views of the Soviet Problem," *New Yorker*, November 2, 1981, p. 62.

21. Ibid. According to Victor Weisskopf, professor emeritus, MIT, a principal member of the Manhattan Project, the United States could unilaterally eliminate all its land-based intercontinental ballistic missiles with no loss of security (lecture to a class, "Science and Values," at the University of Michigan, April 5, 1982).

22. "Last Roundup for NATO," *Bulletin of the Atomic Scientists*, February 1982, p. 7.

23. The Boston Study Group, *Winding Down: The Price of Defense* (New York: W.H. Freeman, 1982), pp. 305, 50.

24. Statement to the Iraqi Cabinet, reported by the Cyprus office of the Associated Press and published in the *Ann Arbor News*.

25. Quoted in Daniel Yergin, "The Terrifying Prospect: Atomic Bombs Everywhere," *Atlantic Monthly*, April 1977, p. 53.

26. Jim Harding, Leonard Ross, and Llewellyn Werner, "Argentina Will Have a Bomb in Three Years," *Ann Arbor News*, May 24, 1982.

27. Article VI of the Treaty reads: "Each of the parties . . . undertakes to pursue negotiations in good faith on effective measures relating to . . . nuclear disarmament, and on a treaty on general and complete disarmament under strict and effective international control."

28. Quoted in Robert Johansen, "Non-Progress in Non-Proliferation," *Sojourners*, September 1980, p. 5.

29. Jonathan Schell, "The Fate of the Earth," *New Yorker*, February 15, 1982, p. 75.

30. The approximate 10,000 figure is based on data supplied by the Center for Defense Information; the Boston Study Group; Andrew Cockburn (author of *The Threat: Inside the Soviet Military Machine*); Les Aspin of the House Armed Services Committee; Hans Bethe, formerly of the Los Alamos Scientific Laboratory; Franklin Long, professor of science and society at Cornell University; and Jerome Wiesner, president emeritus of MIT. Cf. Harvard Nuclear Study Group, "The Realities of Arms Control," *Atlantic Monthly*, June 1983, p. 46: "Each side has roughly 11,000 warheads on weapons with ranges of over 1,000 miles."

31. Jerome Wiesner, lecture at University of Michigan, March 26, 1982. At an international hearing conducted by the World Council of Churches at Amsterdam, November 23–27, 1981, McGeorge Bundy declared that the United States could reduce its nuclear arsenal by 50 percent and still retain an effective deterrent (editorial, *Christianity and Crisis*, January 18, 1982, p. 371). Bundy was special assistant to the President for national security in the Kennedy and Johnson Administrations.

32. "Arms Control Chief Vows U.S. Will Risk Nuclear War," *Ann Arbor News*, January 19, 1983.

33. State of the Union Address, January 23, 1980.

34. Thompson and Smith, p. xxi.

35. Ibid., p. xx.

36. Ibid., pp. xxiii–xxiv.

37. Quoted in Thomas Powers, "Choosing a Strategy for World War III," *Atlantic Monthly*, November 1982, p. 99.

38. Schell, pp. 75–76.

39. Richard Halloran, "Pentagon Draws Up First Strategy for Fighting a Long Nuclear War," *New York Times*, May 30, 1982, p. 1.

40. Jack Anderson, "We Are Weighing a First-strike Option," *Detroit Free Press*, May 19, 1983.

41. Schriever, "Does U.S. Have Too Many Arms?" *U.S. News and World Report*, May 25, 1959, pp 44–45; Ford, "The Button-II," *New Yorker*, April 8, 1985, pp. 49–92.

42. Fred Hiatt, "Air Force Operating Under Policy to Gain Space Superiority, Documents Show," *Washington Post*, reported in *Ann Arbor News*, January 16, 1985.

43. *Foreign Policy*, Summer 1980, pp. 21, 26.

44. Halloran. See also Center for Defense Information, "Recent Reagan Administration References to Nuclear War-Fighting and Winning," March 21, 1982. This report contains fourteen quotations, with an indication of their sources.

45. Michael T. Klare, "The Reagan Doctrine," *Inquiry*, March/April 1984. See also Carl Blumenstein, "Overkill," *Bulletin of the Atomic Scientists*, December 1984, p. 35.

46. *Annual Report*, p. 32.

47. B.T. Feld, "A Note from the Secretary-General," *Pugwash Newsletter*, October 1975, p. 53.

48. Robert Jungk, *Brighter Than a Thousand Suns* (New York: Harcourt, 1958), p. 267.

49. Ibid., p. 171.

50. Ibid., p. 177.

51. Kennedy, pp. 36, 96, 119.

52. David M. Alpern et al., "Reagan's Arms Buildup," *Newsweek*, June 8, 1981.

53. Caspar Weinberger, "Requirements of Our Defense Policy," *Department of State Bulletin*, July 1981, pp. 46–48; George Shultz, U.S. Congress, Senate Foreign Relations Committee, June 15, 1983.

54. "Reagan's Address to Nation on Nuclear Strategy Toward the Soviet Union," *New York Times*, November 23, 1982, p. 4Y.

55. Alexander L. George and Richard Smoke, *Deterrence in American Foreign Policy: Theory and Practice* (New York: Columbia University Press, 1974), p. 62.

56. "Arms Control: Is There Still Hope?" *Daedalus*, Fall 1980, p. 181.

57. Feld, p. 53. The Pugwash Council, named after the location of its first conference in Pugwash, Nova Scotia, has been meeting regularly since 1957. Its aim is to draw on the expertise of its members in seeking to prevent a nuclear holocaust. The most recent gathering was attended by 169 eminent scientists from thirty-seven countries and five international organizations. In 1960, Herman Kahn foresaw the proliferation of nuclear weapons, the continued arms race, and the development of new weapons systems. Referring to the "very serious danger" this would pose "to both the United States and the Soviet Union," he wrote: "There are few who would believe that the kind of world just described could be stable for very long." *On Thermonuclear War* (Princeton, NJ: Princeton University Press, 1960), pp. 501, 521.

58. Cited in Richard Burt, "A New Type of War?" *New York Times*, October 7, 1980, p. 4.

59. "The Myth of Power, The Power of Myth," *Christianity and Crisis*, November 27, 1978. Reprinted in C.A. Cesaretti and Joseph Vitale, eds., *Rumors of War* (New York: Seabury Press, 1982), p. 72. For a historian's explanation of the need to reassess attitudes and policies in view of the changes that occur in the international structure, see Michael Howard, "Reassurance and Deterrence: Western Defense in the 1980's," *Foreign Affairs*, Winter 1982/83, p. 315.

60. Bradford Lyttle, *The Flaw in Deterrence* (Midwest Pacifist Publishing Center, 5729 South Dorchester, Chicago, IL 60637, 1983).

61. See especially Brian Crissey and Linn Sennott, "Analysis and Simulation of a Launch-on-Warning Policy," unpublished manuscript, April 1984.

62. Schell, p. 45.

63. "Disavowing Violence," *Bulletin of the Atomic Scientists*, September 1980, p. 1.

64. Quoted in Jim Wallis, "Bishops Pastoral and Prophetic," *Sojourners*, April 1983, p. 5.

Chapter II.
Reducing the Soviet Threat

1. October 4, 1984.

2. "Exaggerated Fears of a Soviet Threat to the West," February 19, 1984, p. 9.

3. Alternative Defence Commission, *Defence Without the Bomb* (London and Philadelphia: Taylor & Francis, 1983), p. 71. Cf. General Maxwell D. Taylor, former chairman of the Joint Chiefs of Staff: "Even in the favorable circumstance of a quick victory by conventional means, the Soviets would be left with a prolonged occupation of hostile, hungry, war-damaged countries that would require the indefinite presence in Western Europe of a large part of the Soviet army." ("The Reality of the Soviet Threat," in Grayson Kirk and Nils Wessel, eds., *The Soviet Threat: Myths and Realities* [New York: Praeger, 1978], p. 175).

4. "The Global Reach of the Superpowers," *South: The Third World Magazine*, August 1983.

5. Barbara Tuchman, *The March of Folly* (New York: Alfred A. Knopf, 1984).

6. "The Cold War in Europe: 1945–1967," in Neal D. Houghton, ed., *Struggle Against History* (New York: Washington Square Press, 1968), p. 25.

7. "A View from the Kremlin," lecture delivered at the University of Michigan, March 30, 1983.

8. "Can America Manage Its Soviet Policy?" *Foreign Affairs*, Spring 1984, p. 860.

9. "Soviet Geopolitical Momentum: Myth or Menace?" January 1980, p. 1. Cf. Zbigniew Brzezinski, national security adviser to President Carter: "There is no revolutionary move-

ment in the world today which is modeled after the Soviet Union" (lecture at a symposium on New Weapons Technologies and Soviet-American Relations, University of Michigan, November 14, 1984). See also Sanford Gottlieb, *What About the Russians?* (Northfield, MA: Student/Teacher Organization to Prevent Nuclear War, 1982), pp. 19–21.

10. "Living with the Soviets," *Foreign Affairs*, Winter 1984/85, p. 367.

11. "American Perceptions and Soviet Realities," lecture at University of Michigan, March 13, 1984.

12. See Strobe Talbott, "Communism: The Specter and the Struggle," *Time*, January 4, 1982, p. 49; John Bennett, "Soviet Aims and Priorities: The Need for a New Debate," *Christianity and Crisis*, October 19, 1981; Marshall Shulman, "What the Russians Really Want," *Harpers*, April 1984, pp. 64–65.

13. "The New Soviet Challenge," *Foreign Policy*, Summer 1984, p. 123.

14. Thomas Powers, "What Is It About?" *Atlantic Monthly*, January 1984, p. 38. Others have called attention to U.S. responsibility for escalating the arms race: George Kennan, "Address in Accepting Albert Einstein Peace Prize," May 19, 1981; Everett Mendelsohn, in Jane Myers, "One Expert Finds a Place for Rational Optimism," *Ann Arbor News*, March 20, 1980. Mendelsohn is professor of the history of science at Harvard University.

15. Jonathan Steele, *Soviet Power: The Kremlin's Foreign Policy—Brezhnev to Andropov* (New York: Simon & Schuster, 1983), pp. 85–86. See also George Russell, "Making the Best of Deference," *Time*, November 30, 1981, p. 48; Max Jakobson, "Substance and Appearance: Finland," *Foreign Affairs*, Summer 1980, pp. 1034–44; William Steif, "Who's Afraid of Finlandization?" *The Progressive*, February 1982, pp. 44–46.

16. Cited in Sidney Lens, "But Can We Trust the Russians?" *The Progressive*, July 1980.

17. Alan Wolfe, *The Rise and Fall of the Soviet Threat* (Rev. ed.; Boston: South End Press, 1984), pp. 57–58.

18. "We're Hearing It Again: Reds' Sails in the Sunset," *New York Times*, October 14, 1980. Cf. George Kennan, "America's Unstable Soviet Policy," *Atlantic Monthly*, November 1982, p. 80: "The motivations for American policy toward the Soviet Union . . . have represented for the most part not reactions to . . . the Soviet regime but rather the reflections of emotional and political impulses making themselves felt in the internal American scene."

19. Wolfe, p. 2. This committee was founded in 1976 "on the premise that the United States, if it did not build up its defenses, would soon be impotent in the face of Soviet strength." Its members are right-wing conservatives who habitually take a hard line toward the Soviet Union.

20. Richard Barnet, "Lies Clearer Than Truth," *Sojourners*, August 1979, p. 16; Edward Pessen, *New York Times*, November 12, 1982, editorial pages; MacArthur, "Nuclear War: A Frankenstein," in C.A. Cesaretti and Joseph Vitale, eds., *Rumors of War* (New York: Seabury Press, 1982), p. 32.

21. "In Their Lust for Victory," *Los Angeles Times*, August 24, 1980.

22. Barnet, p. 18; Blaker, "Cruise Missiles: The Dutch Point of View," lecture broadcast over WUOM, Ann Arbor, May 30, 1984; for Harriman, see Kenneth Brown, "What About the Threat to Freedom?" in Dale Brown, ed., *What About the Russians?* (Elgin, IL: Brethren Press, 1984), p. 98; for Howard, see Steele, p. 79; for La Rocque, see *Defense Monitor*, 12:3, 1984; Neild, "How to Make Up Your Mind About the Bomb," *Bulletin of the Atomic Scientists*, January 1982, p. 15; Taubman, "Michigan Briefing on Soviet Affairs," lecture at University of Michigan, October 4, 1984; Wiesner, conversation with author, April 4, 1982; Fulbright, "National Security and the Reagan Arms Buildup," in Ronald Dellums, *Defense Sense: The Search for a Rational Military Policy* (Cambridge, MA: Ballinger, 1983), p. 74.

23. "Two Views of the Soviet Problem," *New Yorker*, November 2, 1981, p. 55.

24. "Countdown to Disaster," *Fellowship*, July/August

1980, p. 5.

25. Ibid.

26. Seweryn Bialer, "The Harsh Decade: Soviet Policies in the 1980s," *Foreign Affairs*, Summer 1981, pp. 1006–7.

27. "Which Comes First, Arms Control or Security?" *New York Times*, March 21, 1982, p. E5.

28. George Kennan, "Reflections on Our Present International Situation," address delivered October 22, 1959, printed by Promoting Enduring Peace, Woodmont, CT, p. 4.

29. "Arms Control Options at Turning Point," brochure, U.N. Association, 1977.

30. For listings of these and other Soviet proposals, see Powers, p. 44, and Marta Daniels and Wendy Mogey, *Questions and Answers on the Soviet Threat and National Security* (Philadelphia: American Friends Service Committee, 1981), p. 10.

31. "What the Russians Really Want," *Harpers*, April 1984, p. 63.

32. "Bilateral Negotiations and the Arms Race," *Scientific American*, October 1983, pp. 155–56.

33. "What Happens If SALT Dies?" *Time*, January 14, 1980, p. 19.

34. Jim Garrison and Pyare Shivpuri, *The Russian Threat: Its Myths and Realities* (London: Gateway Books, 1983), pp. 247, 321. Also Elizabeth Pond, conversation with author, October 11, 1983.

35. Singer, "A Fantasy Speech on National Security," *Congressional Record*, March 11, 1981; Cox, "The CIA's Tragic Error," *New York Review*, November 5, 1980, p. 4; Neal, Pamphlet 347, "Promoting Enduring Peace," Woodmont, CT; Scranton and Scowcroft, "Soviets Willing to Listen to New Arms Proposals," Associated Press, reported in *Ann Arbor News*, November 15, 1980.

36. Marta Daniels and Everett Mendelsohn, "New Threats to Nuclear Disarmament," memo written for American Friends Service Committee, October 1979.

37. Ibid.

38. *Congressional Record*, June 27, 1980, p. H5839.

39. Watson, "The Case for SALT II," *Forbes*, November 9, 1981, p. 41; concerning Smith, see "The Arms Race," *Ann Arbor News*, November 7, 1980; John M. Swomley, "The Myths of Soviet Intentions," in Dale Brown, ed., *What About the Russians?* (Elgin, IL: Brethren Press, 1984), p. 69; Moynihan, letter to the editor, *New York Times*, May 6, 1982; Marta Daniels, "Reflections: Reagan's Public Accusation of Soviet Treaty Violations," *Freeze Focus*, May 1984, pp. 7–8; Thomas K. Longstreth, "Report Aims to Sabotage Arms Control," *Bulletin of the Atomic Scientists*, January 1985, p. 30; "Pentagon Rebuts Charges of U.S. Military Weakness," *Defense Monitor*, No. 8, 1980, p. 8.

40. Daniels, "Reflections: Reagan's Accusation," p. 7.

41. Longstreth, p. 30.

Chapter III.
Foreign Policy and Arms Control—
A New Approach

1. Thomas Powers, "What Is It About?" *Atlantic Monthly*, January 1984, p. 42. Cf. Michael Howard, "Reassurance and Deterrence. Western Defense in the 1980s," *Foreign Affairs*. Winter 1982/83, p. 319.

2. Powers, p. 35; editorial, *Bulletin of the Atomic Scientists*, January 1984, p. 2; Solly Zuckerman, *Nuclear Illusion and Reality* (New York: Vintage Books, 1983), p. 134; Marshall Shulman, "What the Russians Really Want," *Harpers*, April 1984, p. 70; Richard Falk, "The Clear and Present Danger of World War III," *Transition*, November 1979, pp. 1–2; W. Averell Harriman, "We Must Demand a New Effort to Prevent Wars," *Ann Arbor News*, January 8, 1984; "The Nuclear Arms Race," *Newsweek*, October 5, 1981, p. 38.

3. "Reagan's Speech on Soviet-American Relations," *New York Times*, January 17, 1984, p. 6.

4. Willy Brandt, "Alternatives," *Bulletin of the Atomic*

Scientists, June/July 1984, pp. 3, 4; Robert Delaney, "Soviets Escalate After U.S. Missiles Deployed," *National Catholic Reporter*, December 16, 1983; "U.S. Discounts Moves by Soviet Subs," Associated Press, reported in *Ann Arbor News*, January 27, 1984; "Admiral Says Soviets Readying New Missile," Associated Press, reported in *Ann Arbor News*, March 1, 1984.

5. "Retaliation Threatened by Soviets," United Press International, reported in *Ann Arbor News*, December 24, 1983.

6. "U.S. Downplays Missile Threat," Associated Press, reported in *Ann Arbor News*, November 26, 1983.

7. "Soviets Aim More Arms at U.S.," Associated Press, reported in *Ann Arbor News*, May 21, 1984. Cf. Brandt, p. 3: "The conservative governments in Bonn and Washington . . . are attempting to gloss over . . . the new threat and to convince us that everything has remained the same. . . . But it is only a matter of time until the new European weapons systems—in the context of some unforeseen . . . crisis—strain our countries' nerves to the breaking point."

8. See Shulman, p. 70.

9. "Foreign Policy: A Tragedy of Errors," *Bulletin of the Atomic Scientists*, June/July 1984, p. 4.

10. *Facing the Threat of Nuclear Weapons* (Seattle and London: University of Washington Press, 1983), p. 27.

11. "Militarizing the Last Frontier: The Space Weapons Race," *Defense Monitor* 12, no. 5 (1983):6.

12. "Shultz Doesn't See Early Pact with Soviets on Limiting Nuclear Weapons in Europe," *Wall Street Journal*, June 16, 1983.

13. "Behind Closed Doors," *Time*, December 5, 1983, p. 19.

14. "Euromissiles as Bargaining Chips? Think Again!" *Christian Science Monitor*, January 13, 1984.

15. Edward L. Rowny, "Soviets Awaiting Concessions, U.S. Arms Negotiator Says," Associated Press, reported in

Ann Arbor News, April 11, 1984: "The Soviets must understand that we will settle for nothing less than a fully and effectively verifiable agreement."

16. "The American View of U.S.-Soviet Arms Control Negotiations," lecture at the University of Michigan, March 8, 1984.

17. "The Arms Control and Disarmament Agency: An Unfinished History," *Bulletin of the Atomic Scientists*, April 1984, p. 14.

18. Zuckerman, p. 118.

19. Harriman.

20. *Annual Report to the Congress: Fiscal Year 1984* (Washington, DC: Government Printing Office, 1983), p. 58.

21. See *Journal of the Federation of American Scientists*, September 1981, for discussion of the views of Eugene Rostow, Edward Rowny, and Alexander Haig. See also *Department of State Bulletin*, July 1981, pp. 46–48; August 1981, pp. 59–64; and October 1981, pp. 30–34.

22. *Fiscal Year 1983 Arms Control Impact Statements* (Washington, DC: Government Printing Office, 1982), p. v.

23. Powers, p. 55.

24. See Elizabeth Drew, "A Political Journal," *New Yorker*, February 20, 1984, p. 132.

25. Independent Commission on Disarmament and Security Issues, *Common Security: A Blueprint for Survival* (New York: Simon & Schuster. 1982).

26. Alternative Defence Commission, *Defence Without the Bomb* (London and Philadelphia: Taylor & Francis, 1983).

27. See especially *The Politics of Nonviolent Action*, 3 vols. (Boston: Porter Sargent, 1971).

28. "Traditional Arms Control Approach May Be Irrelevant," Newhouse News Service, reported in *Ann Arbor News*, May 27, 1984.

29. Robert C. Johansen, *Toward a Dependable Peace: A Proposal for an Appropriate Security System* (New York: Institute for World Order, 1978); Paul Walker, *Seizing the Ini-*

tiative: First Steps to Disarmament (New York and Philadelphia: Fellowship of Reconciliation and American Friends Service Committee, 1983).

30. Osgood, "The Grit Strategy," May 1980, pp. 58–60.

31. Boston Study Group, *Winding Down: The Price of Defense* (New York: W.H. Freeman, 1982).

32. Fred H. Wright, "The $118 Billion-a-Year Hypothesis," *Fellowship*, April/May 1978, pp. 7–9.

33. "Unilateral Initiatives," May 1984, pp. 50–54.

34. Ibid., p. 52. See also Osgood, p. 60.

35. See, for example, *Christian Century*, January 18, 1982, p. 375; Thomas C. Schelling, *The Strategy of Conflict* (New York: Oxford University Press, 1960), p. 53; *An American Strategy for Peace* (Chicago: World Without War Council, 1984).

36. "How to Start Ending the Arms Race," *World Policy Journal*, Fall 1983, p. 87.

37. Alan Wolfe, *The Rise and Fall of the Soviet Threat* (Rev. ed.; Boston: South End Press, 1984).

38. "In War Policy the Public Has a Vote," *Los Angeles Times*, November 11, 1983.

39. *The Nuclear Delusion* (New York: Pantheon, 1982), p. xxviii. See also Robert J. Lifton and Richard Falk, *Indefensible Weapons* (New York: Basic Books, 1982), pp. 245, 264.

Chapter IV.
Can Modern War Be Moral?

1. Sidney Drell, "Arms Control: Is There Still Hope?" *Daedalus*, Fall 1980, pp. 187, 180, 179.

2. David Wood, "Wanted: U.S. Military Is Hurting for a Few Experienced Men," Newhouse News Service, reported in *Ann Arbor News*, October 1, 1984.

3. Jane Myers, "The Bishops Haven't Misunderstood Anything at All," *Ann Arbor News*, November 22, 1982.

4. Michael Walzer, *Just and Unjust Wars* (New York: Basic Books, 1977), p. 257.

5. See Kennan statement in closing pages of chapter III and Lifton reference in accompanying note.

6. Roger Molander, "How I Learned to Start Worrying and Hate the Bomb," *Washington Post*, March 21, 1982.

7. Drell, p. 180.

8. "Can Nuclear Deterrence Last Out the Century?" *Foreign Affairs*, January 1973, pp. 279, 281.

9. Paul Tillich, *The New Being* (New York: Charles Scribner's Sons, 1955), p. 67.

10. "Weapons and Hope: IV-Concepts," *New Yorker*, February 27, 1984, p. 76.

11. Eunice B. Armstrong, letter, *Society for Social Responsibility in Science Newsletter*, September 1960, p. 4. This statement was made by Herman Kahn of the Rand Corporation on a speech-making tour sponsored by the General Electric Company and local host institutions.

12. "Effects of Biological Warfare Agents," *Emergency Manual Guide*, July 1959.

13. R.P. Turco et al., "Nuclear Winter: Global Consequences of Multiple Nuclear Explosions," *Science*, December 23, 1983, pp. 1286, 1290. Also Paul R. Ehrlich et al., "Long-term Biological Consequences of Nuclear War," ibid., pp. 1294, 1299.

14. "Astronomer Sagan Warns of Nuclear Winter Perils," United Press International, reported in *Ann Arbor News*, July 12, 1984; Lewis Thomas and John Adams, letters distributed by Natural Resources Defense Council, August 8, 1984.

15. John Bennett, "Nuclear Deterrence Is Itself Vulnerable," *Christianity and Crisis*, August 13, 1984, pp. 297, 298.

16. *Time*, August 1, 1960, p. 15.

17. *The Challenge of Peace: God's Promise and Our Response* (Washington, DC: National Catholic News Service, 1983), Sec. II, C, and notes 61, 62, 70.

18. Walzer, p. 23.

19. *Humanity in Warfare* (New York: Columbia University Press, 1980), p. 208.

20. Bill Davidson, "Why Half Our Combat Soldiers Fail

to Shoot," *Collier's Magazine*, November 8, 1952 (reprinted as pamphlet, American Friends Service Committee, Philadelphia).

21. Ibid.

22. David Wood, "Vulnerable: Subtle New Forms of Warfare Threaten U.S.," *Ann Arbor News*, March 22, 1984.

23. "Excerpts from Shultz's Address on International Terrorism," *New York Times*, October 26, 1984, pp. 6, A12.

24. Quoted in "Letter to Clergymen," by Harry R. Rudin, emeritus professor of history, Colgate University, November 1984.

25. Alternative Defence Commission, *Defence Without the Bomb* (London and Philadelphia: Taylor & Francis, 1983), p. 47.

26. Richard Halloran, "Pentagon Draws Up First Strategy for Fighting a Long Nuclear War," *New York Times*, May 30, 1982, p. 1; Center for Defense Information, "Recent Reagan Administration References to Nuclear War-Fighting and Winning," March 21, 1982.

27. Michael Getler, "Reagan's Nuclear War Policy Muddled by Rhetoric," *Washington Post*, reported in *Ann Arbor News*, November 23, 1982; Thomas Powers, "Choosing a Strategy for World War III," *Atlantic Monthly*, November 1982, p. 110; Michael T. Klare, "The Reagan Doctrine," *Inquiry*, March/April 1984.

28. This saying, repeated with many variations, can be traced as far back as the Sibylline Oracles (170 B.C.) of Jewish apocalyptic literature. See Georg Buchmann, ed., *Geflügelte Worte* (32d ed.; Berlin: Haude & Spenersche, 1972), pp. 150–51.

29. John Woolman, *The Journal and Major Essays of John Woolman*, ed. Phillips P. Moulton (New York: Oxford University Press, 1971), p. 38.

30. *Disturbing the Universe* (New York: Harper & Row, 1981), as quoted in *Bulletin of the Atomic Scientists*, December 1981, pp. 1, 4.

31. "Our Precarious Balance of Terror," *Together,* May 1960, p. 32.

32. Edna St. Vincent Millay, "Conscientious Objector," in *Collected Poems* (New York: Harper & Bros., 1956), pp. 305–6.

33. Tillich, chap. 20, particularly pp. 153, 157, 158.

34. Tillich, pp. 159–60.

Chapter V.
An Alternative to Military Defense

1. Leo Tolstoy, *The Law of Love and the Law of Violence* (New York: Rudolph Field, 1948,), p. 104.

2. "Reflections on Violence," *New York Review of Books,* February 27, 1969, p. 30.

3. Preface to Frantz Fanon, *The Wretched of the Earth* (New York: Grove Press, 1968), pp. 7–31.

4. Hugh Davis Graham and Ted R. Gurr, *Violence in America: Historical and Comparative Perspectives* (New York: New American Library, 1969), pp. 362, 785–88.

5. *The Challenge of Peace: God's Promise and Our Response* (Washington, DC: National Catholic News Service, 1983), Sec. III, A, 5, c.

6. James E. Creighton and Harold R. Smart, *An Introductory Logic* (5th ed., rev.; New York: Macmillan, 1933), pp. 220–21.

7. Martin Luther King Jr., *The Trumpet of Conscience* (New York: Harper & Row, 1968), p. 75.

8. As quoted in Tolstoy, p. 107.

9. George F. Kennan, "Foreign Policy and Christian Conscience," *The Moral Dilemma of Nuclear Weapons* (New York: Church Peace Union, 1961), p. 69.

10. Immanuel Kant, *Foundations of the Metaphysics of Morals* (Indianapolis: Bobbs-Merrill, 1959), p. 10.

11. Thomas Merton, *Faith and Violence* (Notre Dame, IN: University of Notre Dame Press, 1968), p. 18.

12. "The Uses of Violence," *Christian Century*, April 17, 1968, p. 485.

13. Editorial, "How Gandhi Would Meet the War," *Christian Century*, January 31, 1940, p. 2.

14. Kenneth Boulding, *Stable Peace* (Austin: University of Texas Press, 1978), pp. 115, 66, 99.

15. See Arthur Weinberg and Lila Weinberg, eds., *Instead of Violence* (Boston: Beacon Press, 1965), and Staughton Lynd, ed., *Nonviolence in America: A Documentary History* (Indianapolis: Bobbs-Merrill, 1966).

16. Joan V. Bondurant, *Conquest of Violence: The Gandhian Philosophy of Conflict* (Rev. ed.; Berkeley: University of California Press, 1967). See especially pp. 45, 55, 61, 132–38.

17. David L. Lewis, *King: A Critical Biography* (New York: Praeger, 1970).

18. Eknath Easwaran, *A Man to Match His Mountains* (Petaluma, CA: Nilgiri Press, 1984), pp. 19, 122.

19. Leroy H. Pelton, *The Psychology of Nonviolence* (New York: Pergamon Press, 1974), p. 203.

20. Ronald Schaffer, *Wings of Judgment: American Bombing in World War II* (New York: Oxford University Press, 1985), p. 31.

21. "Americans Mulled Poisoned Food Plan During War," *New York Times*, reported in *Ann Arbor News*, April 19, 1985.

22. Mary McGrory, "Despite Hawks' Boasts, Americans Prefer Peace," *Detroit Free Press*, April 23, 1984.

23. Magne Skodvin, "Norwegian Nonviolent Resistance During the German Occupation," in *Civilian Resistance as a National Defence: Nonviolent Action Against Aggression*, ed. Adam Roberts (London: Pelican Books, 1969), p. 176.

24. B.H. Liddell Hart, "Lessons from Resistance Movements—Guerrilla and Nonviolent," in Roberts, pp. 239–46.

25. Theodor Ebert, "Nonviolent Resistance Against Communist Regimes?" in Roberts, pp. 207–27.

26. Adam Roberts, "Czechoslovakia and Civilian De-

fence," in Roberts, pp. 7–16; Anders Boserup and Andrew Mack, eds., *War Without Weapons: Nonviolence in National Defense* (New York: Schocken Books, 1975), pp. 102–16, 164–66.

27. Charles Kupchan, "Solidarity's Future," *Harpers*, May 1985, pp. 37–40; John M. Swomley, "The Lessons of Solidarity," *Fellowship*, July/August 1985, pp. 15–17.

28. Ebert, p. 227.

29. This and the two preceding quotations are from Easwaran, pp. 16, 17, 19.

30. *Making the Abolition of War a Realistic Goal* (New York: World Policy Institute, 1980), p. 7.

31. "Some Questions on Civilian Defence," in Roberts, p. 356.

ANNOTATED BIBLIOGRAPHY

By NO MEANS exhaustive, this list includes several lesser-known works relevant to each of the chapters.

Alternative Defence Commission. *Defence Without the Bomb*. London and Philadelphia: Taylor & Francis, 1983. A practical, in-depth study of alternative proposals for a nonnuclear defense policy in Britain. Contains a thought-provoking section on a nonviolent defense strategy.

Best, Geoffrey. *Humanity in Warfare*. New York: Columbia University Press, 1980. A history of the development of international laws and conventions covering war, peace, and neutrality, with an evaluation of the effects of legal mechanisms for controlling warfare since World War II.

Bondurant, Joan V., ed. *Conflict: Violence and Nonviolence*. Chicago and New York: Aldine-Atherton, 1971. Wide-ranging essays by well-qualified contributors, dealing with both theoretical and practical issues.

———. *Conquest of Violence: The Gandhian Philosophy of Conflict*. 2d ed., rev. Berkeley and Los Angeles: University of California Press, 1965. A first-rate treatment of Mahatma Gandhi's philosophy and methods.

Boserup, Anders, and Andrew Mack. *War Without Weapons: Nonviolence in National Defense*. New York: Schocken

Books, 1974. A highly recommended, comprehensive study.

Boulding, Kenneth E. *Stable Peace*. Austin: University of Texas Press, 1978. An original contribution by a highly creative thinker. Based on a simple theory of war-peace systems, a multi-faceted policy is proposed for accelerating the process of societal evolution in the direction of stable peace. While the author is fully aware of the dangers of the present world situation, he draws on a lifetime of reflection to provide peacemakers with a basis for optimism.

Brown, Dale W., ed. *What About the Russians? A Christian Approach to U.S.-Soviet Conflict*. Elgin, IL: Brethren Press, 1984. Essays on the Russian people, Americans' fear of Russians, and Christian responses to communism, the Soviet Union's policies, and its people.

Cox, Arthur Macy. *Russian Roulette: The Superpower Game*. New York: Times Books, 1982. A broad survey of U.S.-Soviet relations, with an especially good chapter on the possibility of accidental nuclear war. It contains a commentary by Georgy Arbatov, foremost Soviet expert on the United States.

Daniels, Marta, and Wendy Mogey. *Questions and Answers on the Soviet Threat and National Security*. 1501 Cherry St., Philadelphia, PA 19102: American Friends Service Committee, 1981. Very well done pamphlet; highly recommended.

Douglass, James W. *The Non-violent Cross: A Theology of Revolution and Peace*. New York: Macmillan, 1966. A proposal for nonviolence examined in three contexts: the contemporary world, the church, and the history of human relations.

Drell, Sidney D. *Facing the Threat of Nuclear Weapons*. Seattle and London: University of Washington Press, 1983. An excellent treatment of the technical realities of nuclear weapons, the limitations the weapons impose on policy options, feasible arms control approaches, the contributions

131

of scientists to official policy, and the effect of public opinion on progress in arms control.

Easwaran, Eknath. *A Man to Match His Mountains: Badshah Khan, Nonviolent Soldier of Islam*. Petaluma, CA: Nilgiri Press, 1984. A remarkable biography of a Muslim follower of Gandhi in the struggle for Indian independence. It explodes the myths that nonviolence can be followed only by those who are gentle, that it cannot work against ruthless opponents, and that it has no place in Islam.

Ferguson, John. *The Politics of Love: The New Testament and Nonviolent Revolution*. Box 271, Nyack, NY: Fellowship Publications, 1979. A historical Christian view of nonviolence, including evidence from the New Testament, pacifism in the early church, and the political dimensions of Jesus' ministry.

Ford, Harold, and Francis X. Winters, eds. *Ethics and Nuclear Strategy*. New York: Orbis Books, 1977. A comprehensive survey by experts with a variety of backgrounds.

Garrison, Jim, and Pyare Shivpuri. *The Russian Threat: Its Myths and Realities*. London: Gateway Books, 1983. A thorough discussion of aspects of U.S.-Soviet relations that are plagued by misinformation and misunderstanding. A wealth of historical information and facts on the current situation is presented to dispel the myths.

Geyer, Alan. *The Idea of Disarmament! Rethinking the Unthinkable*. Elgin, IL: Brethren Press, 1982. Contains an especially good chapter on deterrence.

Goodwin, Geoffrey, ed. *Ethics and Nuclear Deterrence*. London: Croom Helm Ltd., and Council on Christian Approaches to Defence and Disarmament, 1982. Essays representing a wide range of perspectives.

Gottlieb, Sanford. *What About the Russians?* Box 232, Northfield, MA 01360: Student/Teacher Organization to Prevent Nuclear War, 1982. An excellent pamphlet setting the record straight on U.S. and Soviet behavior.

Hardin, Russell et al., eds. "Symposium on Ethics and Nuclear Deterrence," in *Ethics: An International Journal of*

Social, Political, and Legal Philosophy, April 1985. A special issue containing eighteen articles (330 pages) by philosophers and academic strategists. The best recent philosophical thinking (with inevitable professional terminology) on this particular question.

Howard, Michael. *War and the Liberal Conscience*. New Brunswick, NJ: Rutgers University Press, 1978. A comprehensive survey by a distinguished British military historian.

Independent Commission on Disarmament and Security Issues. *Common Security: A Blueprint for Survival*. New York: Simon & Schuster, 1982. An international panel of highly qualified experts produced this set of proposals.

Irwin, Bob, and Beverly Woodward. *U.S. Defense Policy: Mainstream Views and Nonviolent Alternatives*. Box 515, Waltham, MA 02254: International Seminars on Training for Nonviolent Action, 1982. A macroanalysis seminar manual. Excellent for study groups.

Johansen, Robert C. *Toward a Dependable Peace: A Proposal for an Appropriate Security System*. 777 U.N. Plaza, New York, NY 10017: World Policy Institute, 1978. A brief, clear proposal for implementing the program of independent initiatives discussed in chapter III.

Johnson, James Turner. *Can Modern War Be Just?* New Haven, CT: Yale University Press, 1984. A moral analysis of contemporary war, with particular emphasis on the just-war doctrine.

Kaldor, Mary, and Dan Smith, eds. *Disarming Europe*. London: Merlin Press, 1982. Essays describing the realities of the nuclear arsenals in Europe and proposals for disarmament and new forms of defense.

Kennedy, Robert F. *Thirteen Days: A Memoir of the Cuban Missile Crisis*. New York: W.W. Norton, 1969. This short, readable account provides a valuable context for understanding the dynamics of a superpower confrontation.

Lifton, Robert J., and Richard Falk. *Indefensible Weapons: The Political and Psychological Case against Nuclearism*.

New York: Basic Books, 1982. Lifton holds the Foundation's Fund Chair for Research in Psychiatry at Yale University; Falk is Milbank Professor of International Law at Princeton University. They explore our psychological, political, and military dependence on nuclear weapons for a security that is illusory, and suggest how awareness of the absurdity of our predicament can impel us to action toward a human future.

Lyttle, Bradford. *The Flaw in Deterrence*. 5729 S. Dorchester, Chicago, IL 60637: Midwest Pacifist Publishing Center, 1983. A long-term student of U.S. foreign policy, Lyttle analyzes the writings of several influential deterrence strategists, showing that they overlook the implication of mathematical probability theory—that given a sufficient time span, our present policy is virtually certain to result in nuclear war. A timely, significant work.

McSorley, Richard. *New Testament Basis of Peacemaking*. Washington, DC: Center for Peace Studies, Georgetown University, 1979. This deals effectively with the chief questions people raise on this subject.

Mische, Patricia. *Star Wars and the State of Our Souls*. Minneapolis: Winston Press, 1985. In addition to an informed critique of the Strategic Defense Initiative, this book advocates specific arms control initiatives, explores Soviet treaty compliance, and supplies a philosophical framework that opens new vistas of a secure world order.

Osgood, Charles E. *An Alternative to War or Surrender*. Urbana: IL: University of Illinois Press, 1962. An exposition of the GRIT proposal discussed in chapter III.

Paskins, Barrie, and Michael Dockrill. *The Ethics of War*. London: Gerald Duckworth, 1979. Using three concrete issues from recent history and contemporary politics, leading British authorities provide an in-depth philosophical discussion.

Report of a working party under the chairmanship of the Bishop of Salisbury. *The Church and the Bomb: Nuclear Weapons and Christian Conscience*. London: Hodder &

Stoughton and CIO Publishing, 1982. An analysis of the technical issues combined with an exploration into the underlying moral questions, plus recommendations for British and NATO policies.

Schaffer, Ronald. *Wings of Judgment: American Bombing in World War II*. New York: Oxford University Press, 1985. A well-documented study of the attitudes of those responsible for U.S. strategic bombing regarding the moral issues involved.

Schwartz, Justin. *What About the Russians?* 410 W. Washington St., Ann Arbor, MI 48103: Michigan Alliance for Disarmament, 1983. A pamphlet. Concise answers to commonly asked questions by a scholar well versed in the philosophical and ideological issues involved, as well as the realities of U.S. foreign policy.

Shannon, Thomas A., ed. *War or Peace?* New York: Orbis Books, 1980. Essays on just-war theory, pacifism, and the relation of the church to pacifism.

Sharp, Gene. *Making the Abolition of War a Realistic Goal*. 777 U.N. Plaza, New York, NY 10017: World Policy Institute, 1981. A prize-winning pamphlet summarizing Sharp's thinking on the practical aspects of civilian-based defense.

————. *Making Europe Unconquerable: The Potential of Civilian-based Deterrence and Defense*. Cambridge, MA: Ballinger Publishing Co., 1985. A comprehensive presentation of the main features of civilian-based defense and its relevance to the needs of Western European nations. Sharp makes a convincing case for serious consideration of this method as an alternative to the present policy of seeking security by military means.

————. *National Security Through Civilian-based Defense*. 3636 Lafayette Ave., Omaha, NE 68131: Association for Transarmament Studies, 1985. A brief introduction to civilian-based defense, which outlines its chief characteristics, suggests ways to raise the public awareness of its potential, and points to areas in which further research and policy studies are needed.

————. *The Politics of Nonviolent Action.* Boston: Porter Sargent, 1973. 3 vols. Pt. I. "Power and Struggle"; Pt. II. "The Methods of Nonviolent Action"; Pt. III. "The Dynamics of Nonviolent Action." A total of more than 900 pages, the classic in the field.

————. *Social Power and Political Freedom.* Boston: Porter Sargent, 1980. Essays exploring the possibility of dealing with a variety of social problems by nonviolent methods. Among the subjects considered are: the nature of political power, civil disobedience, genocide, tyranny, and replacing violent sanctions with nonviolent ones.

Sider, Ronald J., and Richard K. Taylor, *Nuclear Holocaust and Christian Hope.* Downers Grove, IL: InterVarsity Press, 1982. A comprehensive answer to the question "How should Christians respond to the threat of nuclear war?" Contains four chapters that provide a good introduction to nonviolent methods of defense.

Thompson, E.P., and Dan Smith, eds. *Protest and Survive.* New York and London: Monthly Review Press, 1981. Essays on the problems in U.S. military and foreign policy, and the threat of a U.S.-Soviet nuclear war. In particular, the dangers of Pentagon plans for a "theater" nuclear war in Europe are portrayed for the American reader.

U.S. Bishops. "The Challenge of Peace: God's Promise and Our Response," in *Origins: NC Documentary Service,* May 19, 1983. The well-known pastoral letter.

Walker, Paul. *Seizing the Initiative: First Steps to Disarmament.* 1501 Cherry St., Philadelphia, PA 19102: American Friends Service Committee and Fellowship of Reconciliation, 1983. A proposal for independent initiatives that either the Soviet Union or the United States can take individually to achieve disarmament.

Walzer, Michael. *Just and Unjust Wars: A Moral Argument with Historical Illustrations.* New York: Basic Books, 1977. The classic study of the just-war tradition.

Wolfe, Alan. *The Rise and Fall of the Soviet Threat: Domestic Sources of the Cold War Consensus.* Rev. ed. Boston: South

End Press, 1984. Wolfe does a convincing job of demonstrating that the degree of emphasis on the Soviet threat depends more on the cycles of U.S. domestic politics than on Soviet behavior.

Yoder, John Howard. *When War Is Unjust: Being Honest in Just-War Thinking.* Minneapolis: Augsburg Publishing House, 1984. A study of the implications of the just-war tradition and a challenge to Christians who adhere to this tradition.

Zuckerman, Solly. *Nuclear Illusion and Reality.* New York: Random House, 1982. A short survey by a former scientific adviser to the British Ministry of Defence.